Routledge Revivals

Supporting Science and Technology

Published in 1998. The Desirable Outcomes for pre-fives and the National Curriculum for Key Stage 1 set out the requirements for learning from nursery through to the end of Key Stage 1 in both science and technology. This book will increase the confidence of the classroom assistants by offering suggestions for improving their subject knowledge in line with these requirements, and advise on how to support the teacher and the child through appropriate learning activities. The handbook will also benefit headteachers and teachers in early years settings who are training volunteers or classroom assistants (perhaps taking STA, BTEC or NNEB courses).

Supporting Science and Technology
A Handbook for those who Assist in Early Years Settings

Ann Montague-Smith and Lorna Winstone

First published in 1998
by David Fulton Publishers Ltd

This edition first published in 2018 by Routledge
2 Park Square, Milton Park, Abingdon, Oxon, OX14 4RN
and by Routledge
711 Third Avenue, New York, NY 10017

Routledge is an imprint of the Taylor & Francis Group, an informa business

© 1998 Ann Montague-Smith and Lorna Winstone

All rights reserved. No part of this book may be reprinted or reproduced or utilised in any form or by any electronic, mechanical, or other means, now known or hereafter invented, including photocopying and recording, or in any information storage or retrieval system, without permission in writing from the publishers.

Publisher's Note
The publisher has gone to great lengths to ensure the quality of this reprint but points out that some imperfections in the original copies may be apparent.

Disclaimer
The publisher has made every effort to trace copyright holders and welcomes correspondence from those they have been unable to contact.

A Library of Congress record exists under LCCN: 98184565

ISBN 13: 978-1-138-48173-2 (hbk)
ISBN 13: 978-1-351-05987-9 (ebk)
ISBN 13: 978-1-138-48175-6 (pbk)

Supporting Science and Technology

A Handbook for those who Assist in Early Years Settings

Ann Montague-Smith and Lorna Winstone

David Fulton Publishers
London

David Fulton Publishers Ltd
Ormond House, 26–27 Boswell Street, London WC1N 3JD

First published in Great Britain by David Fulton Publishers 1998

Note: The right of Ann Montague-Smith and Lorna Winstone to be identified as authors of this work has been asserted by them in accordance with the Copyright, Designs and Patents Act 1988.

Copyright © Ann Montague-Smith and Lorna Winstone 1998

British Library Cataloguing in Publication Data
A catalogue record for this book is available from the British Library

ISBN 1-85346-513-5

All rights reserved. The materials in this publication may be photocopied for use only within the purchasing organisation.

Typeset by Helen Skelton, London

Contents

Foreword by Hilary Emery — v

Acknowledgements — vi

Introduction — 1

1. Working together — 5
2. Science and design and technology — 15
3. Health and safety — 26
4. Working with children — 39
5. Life and living processes — 51
6. Materials and their properties — 60
7. Physical processes — 69
8. Technology processes — 79

Activity sheets — 92

Bibliography — 104

Useful addresses — 105

Index — 106

Foreword

It is with great pleasure that I write the Foreword to this book. Having had the privilege to teach with both the authors over a number of years I am aware of their ability to communicate effectively and supportively with adults working with early years children. Their ideas are practical, effective and based on a secure understanding of child development, of the needs of early years children and the nature of science and design and technology as set out in the Desirable Outcomes and the National Curriculum.

Assistants working with teachers and early years children have a very important role to play in helping children to develop their understanding of science and design and technology. Much of this development will come through children's play and other activities such as physical education. Assistants can play a key part in identifying this learning and working with teachers to take children's ideas forward. The book will help assistants to feel secure about their own understanding of science and design and technology so that they are confident when talking and working with children. It will help them to introduce children to new ideas and activities in science and design and technology and to extend their existing ideas.

It is a practical guide that can help the teacher or group leader to support classroom assistants in developing their skills, or help assistants who want a practical, readable way to increase their skills and knowledge. It can be used as a stand-alone study guide or in conjunction with study on courses such as the Specialist Teacher Assistant courses, BTEC and NNEB early years training programmes. The photographs of children working on science and design and technology tasks help to bring to life the variety of practical, challenging and enjoyable learning activities suggested throughout the book.

As we go into the new century, the contribution that assistants can make to early years teaching will undoubtedly increase. This book, with its consideration of the place of information communication technology in science and design and technology teaching, will help assistants to be effective members of the teaching team in the classroom.

Hilary Emery
Dean of Education
Worcester College of Higher Education
December 1997

Acknowledgements

Our thanks go to our colleagues at Worcester College of Higher Education who have encouraged and supported us in writing this book. In particular we would like to thank the following: Frank Bristow for reading and commenting on each chapter; for making the taking of photographs such fun, class teacher Gill Woodham, classroom assistant Liz Partridge and the reception class at Lea Street First School, Kidderminster, and class teacher Melanie Marshall, classroom assistant Tracey Ward and the Year 1 class at Pitmaston Primary School, Worcester; David Montague-Smith who took all the photographs for the book and read and commented on the chapters; and Fiona Thompson and Shirley Williams, students at Worcester College of Higher Education, who drew all the illustrations. Finally our thanks must go to our families and friends who have been so encouraging of our efforts.

Ann Montague-Smith and Lorna Winstone
Worcester
December 1997

Introduction

About this book

Science and technology are key aspects of education in a modern, industrial society. Scientists use their understanding to make new discoveries which are used to develop and produce new products, such as in cancer research, space research, and products to be used at home and work. Many adults believe that they know very little about science and technology. This is not true, as so much of the success in our daily lives depends upon our use of what we have come to know and understand and the skills which we have developed.

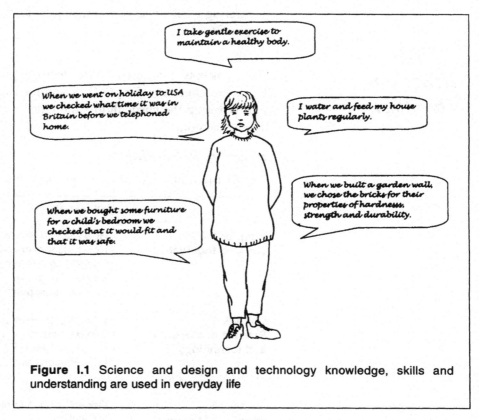

Figure I.1 Science and design and technology knowledge, skills and understanding are used in everyday life

Children begin to develop their scientific and technological understanding from a very early age. Imagine a baby sitting up in a cot. She is playing with a toy that she throws out of the cot. The toy will fall to the ground because of the gravitational pull of the Earth. A young child will repeat the action of throwing toys and will come to realise that they always fall to the floor. This is the beginning of developing knowledge and understanding about forces. Similarly, children explore materials through building with bricks and construction kits, cutting and sticking, spreading paint. They discover some of the ways such materials can be used. By the time children start more formal education, whether at playgroup or nursery or in the reception class at school, they will already have formed their own understanding of how and

Science and technology

why things work. Often they will have formed good concepts, for example knowing that different living things live in different places, such as ponds or woods. Sometimes they will have formed misunderstandings, for example believing that after water is added to dry sand they can dig down to find the water. Children are not 'empty vessels' to be filled up with facts and ideas; they are scientists and technologists in the making who need to develop their understanding through practical activities and discussion with other children and adults.

This book is designed for those who work as an assistant in the classroom, the nursery, at playgroup, with groups or with individual children who have Individual Education Plans (IEPs). It will help assistants to develop children's scientific and technological understanding through:

- building adult confidence with scientific and technological ideas and processes;
- providing support for practical tasks which will enhance adult understanding of concepts and skills;
- offering support with the role of assistant;
- offering teachers advice in using the assistant's support for the children's benefit.

Key concepts for science and technology are considered both for the Desirable Outcomes for pre-fives and for National Curriculum Key Stage 1, thus covering the curriculum requirements for children until they are about seven years old.

Processes in learning

The first four chapters cover issues that permeate the key concepts.

	Key issues
Chapter 1 **Working together**	• How assistants can support teachers. • How teachers can support assistants. • Supporting children, including SEN; English as another language. • Expectations: planning, implementing and evaluating.
Chapter 2 **Science and design and technology**	• What are science and technology? • The relationship between science and technology. • Equality of access to the curriculum. • Investigations and problem-solving.
Chapter 3 **Health and safety**	• General issues to consider concerning science and technology. • Risk assessment. • Using equipment safely and correctly. • Working outdoors.
Chapter 4 **Working with children**	• Finding out about children's ideas in science and technology. • Words which have specific meaning in science and technology. • The use of open and closed questions. • Using language to promote scientific and technological thinking. • Recording outcomes and using IT.

The curriculum

The curriculum content is discussed in Chapters 5 to 8.

	Desirable Outcome Statement	**National Curriculum Programme of Study**
Chapter 5 Life and living processes	Children talk about where they live, their environment [and] their families. They explore and recognise features of living ... in the natural ... world and look closely at similarities, differences, patterns and change. They talk about their observations, sometimes recording them and ask questions to gain information about why things happen and how things work. They use technology, where appropriate, to support their learning.	• Life processes • Humans as organisms • Green plants as organisms • Variation and classification • Living things in their environments
Chapter 6 Materials and their properties	They explore and select materials and equipment. They talk about their observations, sometimes recording them and ask questions to gain information about why things happen and how things work. They use technology, where appropriate, to support their learning.	• Grouping materials • Changing materials
Chapter 7 Physical properties	They explore and recognise features of ... objects and events in the made world and look closely at similarities, differences, patterns and change. They talk about their observations, sometimes recording them and ask questions to gain information about why things happen and how things work. They use technology, where appropriate, to support their learning.	• Electricity • Forces and motion • Light and sound
Chapter 8 Technology processes	They explore and select materials and equipment and use skills such as cutting, joining, folding and building for a variety of purposes. They talk about their observations, sometimes recording them and ask questions to gain information about why things happen and how things work. They use technology, where appropriate, to support their learning.	• Designing skills • Making skills • Knowledge and understanding

Technology is now called 'design and technology' in the National Curriculum and this term is used within this book.

The book is written for assistants and can be used as part of a professional development course or for self-study. There are activities within each chapter for the assistant to carry out, and supporting discussion of likely outcomes. There are notes for leaders of professional development courses at the end of each chapter.

Notes for assistants

It is recommended that you discuss the issues raised in the chapters with another assistant, friend, family member or your class teacher, in order to help you to reflect upon what would help you to set yourself further development targets.

- Read the chapter through, trying each activity. This will help you to develop an understanding of each key concept. Towards the end of the book there are some photocopiable sheets. These relate to specific activities and are designed to help you to record your ideas.
- Decide which activities you would like to adapt for use with children and try these out. Keep a notebook of your observations about children's learning.
- The chapters will help you to be more aware about children's early experiences of science and technology, to build key concepts, help children develop scientific and technological language, record their outcomes and to identify opportunities for using information technology (IT).
- Each chapter contains a section headed 'Supporting understanding'. This includes suggestions of resources to be used with children, and there are further reading suggestions for you as well as, where appropriate, lists of other materials and software to help develop your understanding.

Notes to leaders

☞ Encourage assistants to identify the science and technology knowledge, skills and understanding which they use in everyday life.

☞ Encourage them to share their most positive and negative experiences of learning about science and technology.

☞ Ask them to identify the key influences of these experiences, such as the role of the teacher, the relevance of the experience to their lives, the suitability of the textbook.

☞ Ask them to think back over the previous day and to identify aspects of science and technology which they used. These can be listed under the following headings:
- Life processes and living things
- Materials and their properties
- Physical processes
- Designing
- Making

☞ Encourage assistants to keep notes when working with children. These should include what was planned, the resources used and reflections upon the outcomes for the children's learning.

Supporting understanding

Further reading

DFE (1995) *Key Stages 1 and 2 of the National Curriculum*. London: HMSO.

National Curriculum Council (1993) *Teaching Science at Key Stages 1 and 2*. York: NCC.

School Curriculum and Assessment Authority (1997) *Baseline Assessment Scales*. London: HMSO.

School Curriculum and Assessment Authority (1997) *Looking at Children's Learning: Desirable Outcomes*. London: HMSO.

School Curriculum and Assessment Authority (1996) *Nursery Education: Desirable Outcomes for Children's Learning*. London: HMSO.

School Curriculum and Assessment Authority (1995) *Science: Consistency in Teacher Assessment. Exemplification of Standards*. Key Stages 1 and 2. Levels 1 to 5. London: SCAA.

CHAPTER 1

Working together

This chapter focusses upon ways of working:
- assistants supporting teachers within the classroom;
- assistants supporting children in their learning;
- teachers supporting assistants in successfully carrying out their work;
- expectations and responsibilities of the teacher, the assistant and the children.

As an assistant – supporting teachers

This section is particularly addressed to assistants who may work in one classroom with the same teacher or work in different classrooms with different teachers during the week. Whoever the assistant supports, there should be regular times when the assistant and teacher can discuss their work together. This should include discussions of the teacher's expectations of the assistant when the assistant works in the classroom.

During the discussions the teacher should make clear to you, the assistant:
- what is expected of you;
- the tasks that you are expected to undertake with the children;
- the groups or individuals with whom you are to work;
- how the task is to be carried out, with specific advice when it is needed.

In order to be as efficient and helpful as possible it is important for you to check the following in order to avoid any misunderstandings with the teacher or science and design and technology coordinators in the school:
- where tools, equipment and resources for science and design and technology are kept. This will include being sure that you know how to access the equipment that you will need for preparation before the lesson begins. You will need to know where the equipment is kept, whether you will need to sign it out or can just go and collect what is needed. Also consider how to return it in good order.
- that you have read and understood the school's policies for:
  - health and safety (and see Chapter 3 for further advice). This policy will make explicit how to deal with safety issues and problems that may occur while you are working.
  - science. This policy will advise on approaches to helping children to learn, and on the range of knowledge and skills that will be necessary to help you help the children.
  - design and technology. This will involve you in using many varied materials, tools and pieces of equipment. The policy will help you to understand the processes with which the children will become familiar and the skills which the children will, with your help, begin to develop.
- that you know how to use tools, equipment and resources safely and have considered any difficulties which children may encounter in using these.

(See Chapter 3 for further advice on the safe use of tools, equipment and resources.) You may want to practise using some of the tools which are unfamiliar so that you are quite sure how to use them safely. Ask your teacher for advice, or the relevant subject coordinator, who will be able to show you the correct method for use. Remember: there is everything to be gained from asking for advice; accidents are more likely to happen when the user of tools lacks knowledge or is careless about their use.

- that you know which handwriting style the school uses and that you can write in this way. This will help the children to read any worksheets or information sheets which you prepare for them. Always check that new words are spelled correctly. Alternately, you may wish to use the class computer to word-process worksheets or information sheets. Check with your teacher which she would prefer.

Making a box to hold your pencils

1. Decide what shape of box you want to make. It could be:

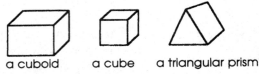

    a cuboid   a cube   a triangular prism

2. Sketch a net for your box. Cut it out and check that it will work.

    This is a net of a cube.

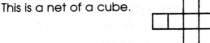

3. Make improvements to your sketch. How will you stick the sides of the box together?
4. Cut out the net from card and make the box.
5. How could you improve your box?

Figure 1.1 You may be asked to make worksheets, either hand-written ones or produced ones using a computer. They must be clear, easy to read, and correctly spelled.

One of the key considerations in building a good relationship with the teacher is to ensure that the lines of communication are strong. Your teacher will appreciate your sensitive approach. Do:

- share information about your particular interests and strengths. For example, you may have a hobby or skill which the teacher would find most beneficial for the children, such as an interest in making your own clothes, or being a keen cook, or perhaps you are particularly interested and knowledgeable about the local wildlife.
- discuss anything you are not sure about or find difficult. This could be a lack of knowledge and understanding about a scientific principle or a lack of confidence in using a new tool or technique in design and technology. Your teacher will appreciate your honesty and desire to learn and will offer advice and support.
- check that you know what you have to do. If you are unsure, then ask. This will help you to feel more confident when you work with the children and to ensure that you are working in the same way as the teacher.
- pass on any relevant observations about individual children. Sometimes you will observe that an individual child has grasped a new concept or

idea, or you will notice that a child has become competent at using a particular tool. Your teacher will be pleased to hear of this and may add this information to her records book. At other times you may be given information about life at home by a child which you also think the teacher should know. You will learn much about individual children; take care to keep this information confidential within the school.
- work under the teacher's direction. The teacher has professional and legal responsibility for the children. You and the teacher will build a working partnership, but within this partnership the teacher has overall management control within the classroom.

Activity 1.1 Working in partnership Use Activity sheet 1 to record and think about your work in the classroom. Identify those things which you know you do well. List aspects of your work with which you feel confident. Think about what makes your work more difficult, or where you need some help. Make a list of these points as well. With your teacher's support, use these lists to guide you in discussing ways in which you can become even more helpful in the classroom.

Discussion Those things which you do well, and those areas where you feel confident, help you to support your teacher and the children in the classroom. Where you need help consider, with your teacher if possible, how this help can be given. You may:
- read up on areas where you feel you do not know enough;
- practise using tools, materials and equipment so that you become more familiar, and so more confident, with their use;
- become more familiar with how the school is organised so that you become more aware of who can help you with very specific questions.

As an assistant – supporting children

As a classroom assistant you are likely to be asked to undertake a variety of different tasks when working with children. These include:
- showing children what to do;
- encouraging children to talk about their work;
- offering constructive feedback;
- helping children with their work;
- working with children with special educational needs;
- working with children for whom English is their second language.

In this section each of the above ways of working will be considered in order to highlight good classroom practice. There are some general points to consider before you begin to work with a group or individuals in the classroom. Always check that:
- you know the purpose of the activity. In planning the activity the teacher will have had a specific learning outcome in mind for the children. It is important to keep that in your mind as you work, so that you can explain to the children the focus of the activity. Children learn best when they know the reason for learning about something.
- you have everything prepared and ready for the activity to begin. This may mean collecting materials from a store, or preparing a space to work in the classroom.
- you have considered the health and safety aspects of the activity and can remind the children of possible safety factors.
- you know the main points which you need to make in your demonstration or explanation.

- you have considered the vocabulary which you will use to introduce or encourage the children to practise in their responses.

Showing children what to do

Perhaps the teacher has asked you to demonstrate to a group of children how to use a cool glue gun safely, or how to collect minibeasts using a spoon without injuring them. Whatever the task, you will want to make the best use of the time and ensure that all the children have understood what it is they have to do. To work effectively while showing children what to do, try to ensure that you consider the following.

- Ensure that all the children can see what you are doing. This may mean re-arranging the furniture, or moving the children to a different place from where they will work. Alternately, you may want to break the group into two smaller ones and demonstrate separately to each.

Figure 1.2 Always make sure that all the children can see what you are doing

- Avoid the children facing other groups of children. This may mean moving from where you had originally intended to work, but you do want to ensure that everyone in the group is listening and watching. Other children's activities may be very tempting for some of your group to watch!
- Make your explanations simple and clear. Ensure that you can be heard by all in your group, but remember you do not want to disturb another group by speaking too loudly. Choose carefully the vocabulary you will use, explain new vocabulary and ask children to repeat new words, and name newly introduced tools, equipment and resources.
- Check that all the children are watching and listening as you demonstrate and explain. Look at the children from time to time and try to establish eye contact with them as this will encourage them to focus upon what you are doing and saying.
- Ask questions as you demonstrate, to check that the children have understood. Such questions include:
  - 'Why am I holding this like this?'
  - 'What would happen if ...?'
  - 'How could I ...?'

- Encourage the children to maintain their interest through asking individuals to choose materials, hold equipment and make measurements for you. This will help to maintain their interest and give you opportunities to check that they have understood the process.
- At the end of the explanation ask individuals to repeat what you said, or demonstrate by showing, so that you can check that they have understood.

Encouraging talk

Children's language development will improve as they are encouraged to discuss their work. This is most effectively done when open questions are used, such as:

- 'What if you ...?'
- 'Why do you think ...?'
- 'What else could you use?'
- 'Is there another way?'
- 'How could you ...?'
- 'What do you think will happen if ...?'

Such questions encourage the children to think about what they are doing and to make changes and improvements to their plans, models or investigations. 'What if?' questions help children to make predictions and to consider ways of making improvements to their work. In scientific investigations children will be encouraged to make and test their predictions and to begin to understand how and why things happen. Encourage the children to ask each other questions about their work so that they use and understand new vocabulary and develop effective and appropriate questioning skills.

Giving feedback

While the children are working you will want to talk with them about what they are doing. Give positive feedback and praise where it is due, but do not praise poor work as children need help and encouragement to achieve high standards of work. Instead, discuss with the child why you believe the work to be poor, and ask him or her what he or she would need to do in order to improve it. For some children, particularly those who find the work difficult or who find concentrating for a long time very demanding, it can help to praise the small, positive steps that they take during the lesson. When giving feedback, be constructive so that children can identify the strengths in their work, and know what they need to do in order to do even better. Ask 'What if?' questions to encourage children to evaluate their own work. When giving feedback try to:

- keep the discussion on the task. Some children may want to engage you in discussion about last night's television. This is not appropriate at this time.
- make time during the lesson to talk with each individual child in the group. Show them that you are interested in them and their work.
- encourage the children to ask and answer questions and to describe what they are doing. Listening to their talk will give you information about their level of understanding and confidence with the task.
- use appropriate scientific and technological vocabulary, in context, so that the children hear the words pronounced and used correctly.

Helping children with their work

When the children are ready to begin their task, you will want to be able to respond to their requests for help. Children should be encouraged to develop independence and to take responsibility for their own actions. You can best help them to succeed by:

- encouraging independence. As far as possible, encourage children to make choices of materials, or methods for investigation, for themselves. If they need resources, encourage them to collect them and put them away for themselves. This way of working will be part of the school's policy of helping to develop independence in young children.
- putting out a range of materials, tools and resources from which the children can make their own choices to encourage them to take responsibility for themselves and make their own decisions.
- using the correct vocabulary as you describe tools, materials and resources, so that children hear these words used appropriately.
- reminding the children of any safety considerations, and checking that they remember how to use tools and equipment which they have used previously.
- encouraging accurate, careful working when making models, taking measurements for investigations or writing a report.
- when someone is 'stuck', not doing the work for the child. Instead, offer to demonstrate the skill, using a spare piece of the material, or talk through the problem, so that the child feels confident to try again.
- being aware that all the children have a right of equal access to the curriculum, and the activity offered. Everyone, regardless of gender or race, should have equal access to the materials. Sometimes boys will dominate an activity, especially if construction kits are being used. Similarly, where an activity is seen as being 'female' work, such as sewing, girls may dominate, or the boys may show reluctance to take part.
- encouraging the children to keep their workspace organised and tidy as they work. This helps them to build good life habits. It also has safety considerations, as well-organised workspaces have tools, resources and equipment laid out carefully and safely.

Towards the end of the lesson, you will begin to think about clearing up. Make sure that there is enough time left for the children to clear up, even if they have not finished the task. Children should:

- know where equipment is stored and take responsibility for putting it away safely;
- know where to put their work, finished or unfinished, and clearly marked with their name;
- each take responsibility for an aspect of clearing up, so that everyone is involved. For example, one child could collect the magnifying glasses and put those away, while another could collect the items which were studied. Another child could wipe the table top if this had been dirtied.

Working with children with special educational needs

It is most likely that within the class there will be one or two children who have special educational needs (SEN). The teacher will offer guidance on the nature of the special needs and how the children should be supported in the classroom. It could be that a child has a physical disability, such as partial sight or impaired hearing, in which case the child may need to use special equipment to enhance their sight or hearing. It could be that a child has a condition which affects their motor control, such as cerebral palsy or spina bifida, where the child will need support with writing, and may use a specially adapted computer keyboard for writing. Maybe you are asked to work with a child who has delayed language development, or has difficulty with reading and writing. Whatever the reason for the child needing extra support, the teacher will have information about the condition and will be able to offer specific help and guidance on how to work most effectively to help the child. If you are asked to work with a child with special educational needs always ask the teacher about the child's needs and how these are best supported.

Children who have learning difficulties may need one-to-one support, so you may be asked to work with this child for a part of each day. You may find some or all of the following advice helpful in supporting the child:

- if the child does not understand how to approach the task, try to break it down into smaller steps so that there are opportunities for success with each small step;
- provide encouragement as the child works;
- demonstrate skills, talking through each step with the child;
- encourage discussion, so that the child has the opportunity to use and understand new vocabulary;
- give praise when it is due, for each small step towards success;
- build a positive relationship with the child so that they feel safe and secure when working with you.

Working with children who use English as a second language

In nurseries and schools where there are many children from particular cultures, there may be adults who speak the children's home language who can offer specific help when it is needed. In most nurseries and schools the support for those who speak English as a second (and sometimes third) language will come from the adults and other children within the class. If asked to work with children who are not yet fluent with English ask the advice of the teacher, who may have some specific guidance or programmes of work for the children to follow. When working with children who use English as a second language:

- work alongside the teacher to plan how to support the children;
- encourage language development by explaining the task as you demonstrate, so that the vocabulary you use is heard in the context of what to do;
- encourage the children to repeat new words;
- encourage the children to use their growing English vocabulary to discuss their work;
- offer praise when it is due for each small step of success;
- build a positive relationship with the child so that they feel safe and secure when working with you.

Activity 1.2 Supporting children With your teacher's support, plan a session with a small group or an individual child. In your plan list all the materials, tools and equipment that you will need. Make a list of new vocabulary that you will use. Decide how you will demonstrate the task and make a list of key questions that you will ask. After you have carried out this session make notes on your plan to show what went well, and identify areas where you could improve.

Discussion It is important to plan each session, even if there is not always time to make a written plan. Planning helps to identify what you will do and why, and to have everything ready before the session starts. It also helps to identify the new vocabulary that will be used, in case some new vocabulary is unfamiliar.

As a teacher – supporting assistants

This section addresses the issues of how the teacher can support the assistant. Sometimes assistants will work in just one class; sometimes they will use their time and expertise in a number of classes, so that they work with more than one teacher during each day. Although this section is mainly addressed to the teacher, both of you would find it helpful to read it then discuss how you can work together to improve your partnership in the classroom.

Working together

Assistants work under the guidance and support of the class teacher. The success of the assistant very much depends upon a shared understanding of the roles that each will take. When working with an assistant it is worth making time to talk through how you will both make the partnership work. The successful partnership between teacher and assistant depends upon their trust and respect for each other's work within the classroom.

- Expectations of each other must be made clear. You will be working as a team in the classroom, with you, as the teacher, having overall professional and managerial responsibility.
- Make a regular time to meet for planning. This will ensure that the assistant knows who she will work with, when and the purpose of the task.

There are three key steps to success in the classroom partnership – 'plan, do and review'.

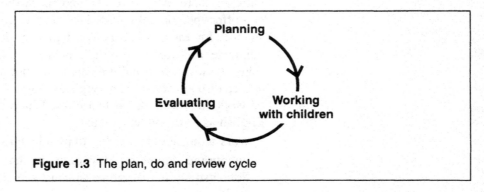

Figure 1.3 The plan, do and review cycle

Planning together

Involving the assistant in the planning process will help her to understand the purpose of what is being planned. This also helps the assistant to see where her specialist knowledge and skills can be used to best advantage. During the planning meeting there will be opportunities to:

- identify where the resources are kept and what will be required.
- agree the procedures for the collection and return of resources.
- list the vocabulary to be developed and agree how it should be used.
- discuss the specific skills and knowledge to be developed by the assistant.
- agree where the assistant will work with the children.

12

- plan the timetable for the week's work so that the assistant will be able to ensure all her preparation is completed in time. She will need to know which children she will support and when.
- identify any children with special needs so that the assistant knows who needs help and support and how to carry this out.
- ensure that you give feedback to the assistant so that the assistant is aware of the effectiveness of her work. Where there are opportunities for improvement agree how this can be done.
- allow time for the assistant to make observations about individual children. Agree what is to be done and by whom. These observations may well contribute towards the assessment and profiling records of the children.

Working with children

The assistant should feel comfortable working in the classroom. The following points will help the assistant to feel valued by you and by the children:

- treat the assistant as a fellow professional in the classroom so that all in the school respect and show value for the skills which she offers;
- ensure that the assistant has an appropriate space to work with the children, so that the children have enough room and suitable furniture to help them to produce good quality work;
- provide sufficient time for the activity, so that the assistant can ensure that all that you planned together is achieved.

Figure 1.4 Make time each week for discussion

Evaluating together

During the time that you set aside together each week, use some time to evaluate the effectiveness of the previous week's planning. This will give the assistant the opportunity to discuss any aspect of her work where she needs support and for you, the teacher, to give positive feedback and encouragement. Do:

- take time to review together the effectiveness of the previous planning and use the review to inform future planning.

- help and encourage the assistant to perceive the positive contribution which she makes to the children.
- ensure that there is a comfortable working atmosphere between you so that the assistant feels safe to discuss any difficulties which she has encountered.
- make time for the assistant to discuss any individual children's achievements.
- make time to identify any individual needs and agree how to meet these in future planning.

Activity 1.3 Working partnerships Review together, teacher and assistant, your current working practices and decide how these could be improved. Make a written agreement between you showing how you will work together.

Discussion Making an agreement on how you intend to work together is a helpful way to begin to strengthen your classroom partnership. Try to arrange a meeting at least once a week, so that you have time to discuss anything which has arisen. Where the assistant works permanently in the classroom it may be possible to meet for a few minutes on a daily basis so that information is exchanged on a regular basis and that planning can be modified in the light of any observations.

Notes to leaders

- Where possible, arrange a session where the teacher and the assistant can work together.
- Encourage the assistants to make written plans for their work with children.
- Where there are two or more assistants working in a school they can be encouraged to form a support group and to help each other with planning.
- Using a science or design and technology activity, ask the assistants to work in pairs to plan this in detail for a small group of children. Encourage them to consider resources, vocabulary, and how they will carry out the task with the children.

Supporting understanding

Further reading

Bentzen, W. (1997) *Seeing Young Children: A Guide to Observing Behaviour*. New York: Delman Publishers Inc.

Crawford, M., Kydd, L. and Riches, C. (eds) (1997) *Leadership in Teams in Educational Management*. Buckingham: Open University Press.

Fox, G. (1993) *A Handbook for Special Needs Assistants: Working in Partnership with Teachers*. London: David Fulton Publishers.

Moyles, J.R. (1992) *Organising for Learning in the Primary Classroom*. Buckingham: Open University Press.

CHAPTER 2

Science and design and technology

This chapter considers the similarities and differences between science and design and technology. The specific issues considered are:
- what are science and design and technology;
- science and design and technology, Desirable Outcomes and the National Curriculum;
- investigations and problem solving;
- gender and learning about science and design and technology.

Science

What is science?

Many adults will have difficulty in recalling scientific experiences from their own primary school days because these will have been very limited. Before the introduction of the National Curriculum schools could choose how much time their pupils spent on scientific activities. In many primary schools the 'nature table' was often part of the classroom and the activities presented by the teachers were mainly those with a biological bias such as growing seeds and keeping frogspawn. Aspects of physics and chemistry were left until the secondary school where there would often be a gender bias, with girls studying biology and boys studying physics and chemistry. This meant that many female early years teachers did not fully appreciate the scientific importance of the experiences that they were already providing in the classroom. The traditional nursery activities such as exploring sand and water enhance the development of scientific ideas as well as being enjoyable.

Science was included as a core subject when the National Curriculum was introduced because it was decided that all children should be given the opportunities to develop scientific understanding from an early age. Society needs future citizens who can appreciate and evaluate the claims made by those responsible for researching and developing new products and processes. To do this effectively people need to have a basic understanding of science.

Scientists put forward theories about how and why things happen and then develop models which help them explain their theories. They produce hypotheses or ideas that can be tested. There may be a number of different theories and models about a particular phenomenon and scientists will often disagree about the 'best' one. The accepted view of a particular phenomenon may also change over time as new theories are proposed. The science studied in nursery and school relies on a body of scientific knowledge already developed. However, science teaching and learning is not just a matter of passing on facts. Experiences of secondary science before the National Curriculum sometimes left pupils feeling that their efforts were not appreciated unless they got the 'right' answer in practical work. To enable the pupils to work in a scientific way they need to be able to carry out practical activities and investigate the scientific ideas at their own level. Science is about using the necessary skills to work in a 'scientific manner' to increase their knowledge and understanding of the world.

Early years science is concerned with fostering the skills and attitudes which enable children to gain a knowledge and understanding of scientific ideas. The requirements outlined at the beginning of the Programmes of Study for science at Key Stage 1 are helpful in suggesting ways in which these can be achieved:

- by encouraging children to work in a systematic way thinking about why things happen;
- by providing children with relevant first-hand experiences that show how science is part of their everyday life;
- by encouraging children to formulate questions and talk with an adult and their peers about their experiences;
- by providing scientific vocabulary when appropriate to encourage children to express their ideas;
- by allowing children to use different ways in which to present their scientific information to others;
- by providing opportunity for children to use IT as appropriate;
- by encouraging children to respect living things and the environment;
- by ensuring children show due regard for their own health and safety.

The National Curriculum for science has two strands:
- 'doing science', the skills of planning experimental work, obtaining evidence and considering evidence, shown in the section called 'Experimental and investigate science';
- the knowledge and understanding of ideas and concepts in the three sections called:
  - 'Life processes and living things';
  - 'Materials and their properties';
  - 'Physical processes'.

The 'doing' of science, and the knowledge and understanding are not separate. Children use their knowledge and understanding of science to carry out activities. In 'doing' the activities they further develop their knowledge and understanding.

Looking for small animals in the school grounds

A Year 2 class carried out work on small animals. This was introduced by the teacher using photographs and videotape of a variety of insects and other small creatures that are commonly found in and around the home and school. She encouraged the children to use the common names of these creatures such as fly, spider, ant and butterfly. The children made a list of the different animals they had heard about. In looking at the pictures the children noticed that, as well as a variety of different animals, there were also different kinds of one particular type, such as different coloured butterflies. This led to the children looking in books and on a CD-ROM to find the names of these different types.

The teacher then introduced the idea that some of these animals might live in the school grounds and encouraged the children to consider where they might find them. The teacher discussed whether it was a good idea to catch these tiny animals and remove them from their 'homes'. The children thought that this would not be necessary unless they found something that they could not name. In this case, they might need to bring the animal inside to look at it more closely and use the books to help them to identify it. The class discussed the kindest ways to collect the animals and the need to return them safely to their homes. They also talked about their own safety when working outside the classroom. The teacher arranged for small groups of pupils to look for small animals with the classroom assistant. Before setting out, the children had to explain to the assistant where they thought they might find the animals, and how they were going to identify them. The teacher provided each group with pictures of the commonest animals as a reminder. The children were encouraged to draw and write about what they had found and make simple charts or graphs to show how many animals they had found. Their work was used as part of a large display and the children talked about what they had found to the Year 4 pupils who visited their classroom.

In the above example the children learnt (acquired knowledge) about:
- a variety of small animals and what they look like;
- where small animals may be found;
- how small animals live.

They developed skills in:
- using secondary sources such as photographs and books to gain information;
- planning the activity to find small animals;
- observing and drawing;
- recording their findings;
- discussing their results;
- collecting small animals without harming them;
- working safely outside the classroom.

They understood:
- that there may be a variety of small animals in the school grounds;
- that these animals can be found in different places.

Equipment used in science

Much of the equipment used for science in schools is shared with other areas of the curriculum such as mathematics and design and technology. Children should have access to:
- measuring equipment including rulers, tape measures and jugs;
- sand-timers and stopwatches for measuring time;
- plastic containers of various kinds, including reclaimed items such as ice cream tubs;
- electrical bulbs, wires and batteries, which will also be needed in design and technology;
- magnets, and a selection of items including nails, paper fasteners, wood, plastics, for investigating the properties of magnetism;
- hand lenses for close observation of objects;
- consumable items such as cooking ingredients which need to be renewed regularly.

Educational catalogues contain equipment for science, including kits for teaching a particular topic. Although these kits often seem expensive they save considerable time in selecting suitable equipment and often contain a selection of teaching ideas. Schools may also have collections of items that they have collected for particular activities.

Design and technology

What is design and technology?

The nursery and primary curriculum has included components of design and technology for many years. It has been called by many different names, such as sewing, junk modelling, woodwork, cooking, cutting and sticking and model making. However, the National Curriculum has extended and enhanced the role of design and technology within the curriculum, so that it now includes:

- designing products, structures and models for a specific purpose;
- making the product, structure or model;
- evaluating what has been made in order to improve its effectiveness;
- learning about the made world;
- studying products that have been made in order to find out how they work and how they were made;
- evaluating the usefulness of a product designed for a specific purpose.

Teddy bear's picnic

Today in school children are encouraged to design, make and evaluate products, structures and models. For example, children in a Year 1 class had decided with their teacher to hold a teddy bear's picnic and to design, make and evaluate some sandwiches for the picnic. The teacher introduced this work with a discussion about bread, the raw ingredients and how bread is made, and every child then experienced making bread for themselves, so that they all learnt about the raw ingredients and how these changed during the making process to become bread. The teacher also brought into class some examples of different types of bread and she and the children discussed which ones would be suitable for making into sandwiches. Each child designed their sandwich, having chosen the bread and filling, and drew a picture of the finished sandwich to show how it would look. Working in small groups with a classroom assistant, children made their sandwiches, following their design. At the picnic a sandwich tasting competition was held and each child completed a brief questionnaire to evaluate each sandwich, to choose their favourite, and explain why they liked that one best.

In the above example, children learnt (acquired knowledge) about:
- the raw ingredients that make bread;
- how bread is made;
- the changes that occur during the cooking of dough to change it into bread;
- hygiene rules for working with food;
- safety rules for using sharp knives.

They developed their skills in:
- designing;
- drawing pictures to show their ideas;
- using a knife;
- making informed choices;
- evaluating products.

They understood:
- how bread is made;
- how they could have improved their own sandwich.

Materials used in design and technology

Many different types of material are used in school. These include:
- paper, card and reclaimed materials such as used commercial packaging;
- fabrics and threads used for sewing, embroidery and in collage work;
- plastic, wood, construction kits and malleable materials such as clay and papier-mâché;
- foodstuffs used in cooking;
- mechanisms such as wheels, pulley and gears, and simple electrical circuits made from bulbs, bulb holders, wire and low voltage batteries.

Children will become familiar with a range of tools and fixings, and learn how to use them safely, including scissors, cool glue guns and handsaws. At all times they will be reminded about health and safety issues; these are discussed in detail in Chapter 3.

Life in the twentieth century

So much of what we use and do in our lives is very different from how it was a hundred years ago. For example, most people in Britain have travelled long distances, even visiting another country; entertainment is provided directly to our homes through the television and video. Children are used to modern life; they were born into this. The rate of change in the technology which is used in everyday life is very rapid, with many homes now owning their own computer which is much more powerful than those used in research 30 years ago. Schools are required to prepare children for adult life, whatever changes that may include, and this makes the role of design and technology in the curriculum even more important as children learn to use modern materials, tools and equipment and to evaluate products which they use in everyday life. This is all part of the preparation for adult life.

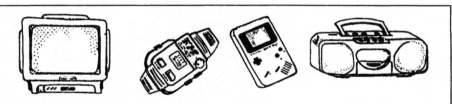

Figure 2.1 Children use devices in everyday life which were unthinkable only a few years ago

The relationship between science and design and technology

Scientific learning helps children to begin to understand the world around them. It helps them to develop their ideas about what happens and to begin to ask why this might be. In science they study natural things and natural phenomena such as electricity, magnetism, light and heat, and in doing this they will form hypotheses by asking themselves questions, testing these out by carrying out investigations and seeking an explanation of their observations.

In design and technology children use materials from the world around them to design, make and evaluate products. They may use scientific knowledge in making their designs, and will learn new skills and practise those they already have learnt in carrying out their designs. They may use their knowledge about electricity, for example, to solve problems in designing and making an electrical circuit to operate lights in a dolls house, installing the circuit, checking that it works and then in evaluating how effective their lighting is.

Science and design and technology have a close relationship. In science children investigate and experiment to test out their ideas, or hypotheses. In design and technology they will use their scientific knowledge in order to solve problems. Table 2.1, compiled from Harlen (1985) and The Design and Technology Association (DATA, 1996), contrasts the processes for each.

Table 2.1 The close relationship between science and design and technology

Science	Design and technology
Using the specifically scientific skills of investigating and experimenting to test ideas.	Using the specifically design and technology skills of devising ways to solve problems.
Generating and testing scientific ideas.	Designing and making a product, using the skills of making and knowledge about materials.
Reflecting critically on the way evidence has been gathered and used in testing ideas.	Evaluating the finished product, looking at ways in which it could be improved.

What children learn

In studying science and design and technology, children acquire knowledge, skills and understanding through studying key concepts. Knowledge, skills and understanding and key concepts are defined in the Desirable Outcomes for Children's Learning and in the National Curriculum Programmes of Study. They are also expected to acquire positive attitudes towards these two subjects.

The Desirable Outcomes for Children's Learning on entering compulsory education

These set out what should be taught to children who are not yet five years old, in nurseries, playgroups, day centres and reception classes, where government funding is provided to pay for the child's place. Science and design and technology is included in the section 'Knowledge and understanding of the world'. This refers to:

- exploration of living things, objects and events in the natural and made world;
- similarities, differences, patterns and change;
- discussion of observations, sometimes recording them and asking questions to gain information about why things happen and why things work;
- exploration and selection of materials and equipment;
- use of skills such as cutting, joining, folding and building for a variety of purposes.

During their first term at mainstream school, baseline assessment will be used to identify children's current knowledge, skills and understanding and then to plan for their entry into the National Curriculum Programmes of Study.

The National Curriculum Programmes of Study

These set out what should be taught to children aged 5 years and over. Children aged 5 to 7 years are taught from the Programmes of Study for Key

Stage 1, and from 7 to 11 years from those for Key Stage 2. There are separate sections for science and for design and technology. Throughout their schooling children are assessed by their teachers so that their knowledge, skills and understanding in these and the other subjects can be recorded and used to plan the next stage of learning.

Knowledge and understanding

In science children are expected to develop knowledge and understanding in:
- 'Life processes and living things': life processes; humans; plants; variation and classification; living things in their environment;
- 'Materials and their properties': grouping materials; changing materials;
- 'Physical processes': electricity; forces and motion; light and sound.

In design and technology children are expected to develop knowledge and understanding about:
- mechanisms: to use simple mechanisms that allow movement;
- structures: how to make structures more stable and withstand greater loads;
- products and applications: investigating simple products and finding out how they work; considering the purpose of the product and how it works; how materials and components have been used; people's needs and what they say about the product;
- quality: how well a product is made and how well it fits its purpose;
- health and safety: simple knowledge and understanding of health and safety, as consumers, and when working with materials;
- vocabulary: using and understanding the appropriate vocabulary.

Activity 2.1 Getting to know the Programmes of Study
Choose either the National Curriculum Programmes of Study, or the Desirable Outcomes if you work with children who are not yet five years old. Read through the Programmes of Study for science and for design and technology. Make a note of anything that surprises you or any aspects with which you are not familiar.

Discussion Where you identify anything that surprises you, talk to your teacher about this and ask them to explain why this aspect is important. There may well be aspects of the Programmes of Study with which you are not familiar. You will find detailed help in Chapters 5 to 8.

Skills

In both science and design and technology children acquire skills which they use in experimental work, investigating and problem-solving.

Science

In science these skills are concerned with 'doing' science:
- planning experimental work: making ideas into a form that can be investigated; thinking through what may happen; recognising when a test is unfair;
- obtaining evidence: using appropriate senses; making observations and measurements; making a record of observations and measurements;
- considering evidence: communicating what happened; presenting results using data handling techniques; making simple comparisons; using results to draw conclusions; indicating whether or not the evidence supports any predictions made; trying to explain what was found out, using existing knowledge and understanding.

Children enjoy practical work in science and the skills gained are of equal importance to the knowledge and understanding of the biological, chemical and physical processes studied. There are different kinds of practical work and children should have opportunities to participate in all of them.

- *Basic skills.* Children need time to learn and practise basic skills such as measuring the same quantity of water into a number of cups or recording results in a simple graph.
- *Demonstrations.* The teacher or another adult might need to demonstrate a practical activity because it is too dangerous for the pupils to carry out. Activities of this type are generally not suitable for primary children, although there may be some aspects of cooking activities that could be included in this section such as removing hot food from an oven. A demonstration may also be used as a starting point for further work.
- *Illustrations.* The teacher may want each child to follow her instructions to illustrate a particular phenomenon. It can be a good way to provide all the children with a starting point for further work. If a class was investigating 'playdough' they might all follow the standard recipe before making their own suggestions for changing the ingredients.
- *Explorations.* First-hand experience of exploring and playing with certain objects enable the children to find useful information about those items. The choice of the objects should be made by the adult initially to ensure that the activity is safe so that the children can explore at their own level. Work on magnetism could begin with exploration by giving the children a pair of magnets and a collection of objects from the classroom.
- *Investigations.* There should be opportunities for children to practise the component parts of planning, obtaining and considering evidence so that on occasions the whole process of investigating an idea is carried out by themselves.

What is an investigation?

During an investigation children apply and develop their knowledge about scientific concepts and skills. They make decisions about 'doing' science in relation to the area that they are studying. Children who are given support in planning and carrying out investigations will become familiar with the different aspects of the process and should eventually be able to carry out the whole investigation by themselves. Adult support can be invaluable in helping children to formulate and carry out investigations. Children's investigations can arise from play, exploration, chance events, discussions and from new science learning. When a teacher plans science work the opportunities for investigations should be shown in that planning together with the focus on the particular aspect of the investigational process.

> **What do snails eat? An investigation**
>
> While a Year 2 class were working on the topic 'Animals' many of the children had found snails in the school grounds. The children noticed that the snails were stuck on walls, between flowerpots and under old logs. They sometimes saw the remains of slime trails near to where the snails were hiding and wondered if the snails moved around at night. Some of the children said that their parents and grandparents complained about the snails in their own gardens and blamed them for holes in the lettuces. This led to one of the children asking the question 'What do snails eat?' Their teacher saw this as an excellent opportunity for some investigations.

The teacher suggested that they collect some snails and keep them in covered plastic tanks in the classroom. She made sure that this would not harm the snails or the children and discussed the care of these animals with the children. Each group of children had different ideas about what the snails might like to eat, but many children included lettuce, grass, dandelions and daisies in their list because they were familiar with those plants. They discussed how the tests could be fair. Some groups put all the foods into the tank each day and looked at the amount of each left the following day. Other groups suggested using the same number of snails and the same amount of food for each test but only using one food at a time. The teacher helped the children to think about how they were going to represent their findings to the rest of the class. They produced drawings and text to describe what they had done. Their results were presented in various ways by using tables and graphs.

Activity 2.2 Investigating toy cars Investigate toy cars running down a slope onto a level track. Which car goes fastest? Which goes furthest? What happens when the gradient of the slope is changed?

Working with children This is an investigation which children will enjoy. Encourage them to think about fair testing, that is, ensuring that only one variable is changed so that it is possible to compare like with like and to see the effect of changing just one variable, such as the gradient of the slope.

Design and technology

In design and technology these skills are:
- designing: drawing upon experience to generate new ideas; clarifying ideas through discussion; developing ideas through shaping, assembling and rearranging materials and components; developing and communicating ideas through drawings and modelling; making suggestions about how to proceed; considering design ideas as they develop and identifying strengths and weaknesses.
- making: selecting materials, tools and techniques; measuring marking out, cutting and shaping; using simple finishing techniques; making suggestions about how to proceed; evaluating the product as it is developed, identifying strengths and weaknesses.

What is problem solving?

In design and technology, children are expected to solve problems. In doing so they learn new skills, practise those that they have already learnt, and have opportunities to develop their knowledge and understanding. In problem solving, the problem will often be set by the teacher, but not always, because children may well identify a problem and consider possible solutions.

Children may decide to design and make a car garage using a construction kit. They will discuss their ideas, taking into account the properties of the construction kit, consider the shape and size that they want to make and draw a sketch of how the garage might look. As they begin to build it they will check as they work, to make sure that it is a suitable size and shape, and check that the car will pass through the door of the garage. They will evaluate the finished garage for its fitness for purpose.

Containers for tennis balls: a problem to be solved

Problem solving encourages children to evaluate what they are doing, while they are doing it. For example, some Year 3 children were asked to make a container large enough to hold three tennis balls so that they did not rattle inside the box. The children considered how they could solve this. They considered the materials that they might use, their properties and suitability for making the box. When they had drafted a design for the box they considered how it could be improved. As they made the box, they evaluated the process, considering as they worked whether the box was of the right size, whether the balls fitted snuggly without rattling, and how they could improve on what they were making. When the box was complete and tested, they evaluated what they made and considered whether it solved the problem. During the making process they were taught new skills in order to carry out the task.

Activity 2.3 Making timing devices Make a sand timer which will time one minute.

Working with children Children may have used traditional sand timers in school and so will have some understanding of what is meant by a timer. If you try this activity, encourage the children to think of possible ways in which they might make a sand timer. Some ideas for this would include pouring sand through a funnel and tubing or making a sand timer from a lemonade bottle.

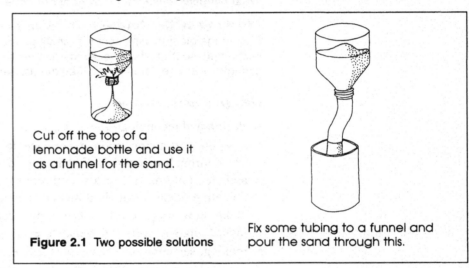

Figure 2.1 Two possible solutions

Cut off the top of a lemonade bottle and use it as a funnel for the sand.

Fix some tubing to a funnel and pour the sand through this.

Developing positive attitudes

Developing positive attitudes in the children for science and design and technology comes through encouragement and support of their interest. Attitudes to foster and encourage include:
- fascination with science and design and technology;
- interest in what they are doing;
- motivation and interest so that they continue with the activity;
- pleasure and enjoyment from the activities;
- appreciation of the purpose and relevance of science and design and technology;
- satisfaction derived from a sense of achievement;
- confidence in an ability to engage with science and design and technology.

Gender and learning about science and design and technology

Today most people believe in equality of opportunity for both boys and girls: that is that boys and girls should have the same opportunities and experiences so that they have equal access to all aspects of learning. In nurseries and primary schools this is regarded as a fundamental right. This may be very different from the memories of adults, who may have attended a school where girls studied domestic science whilst the boys were taught woodwork, or perhaps girls studied biology whilst the boys studied physics and chemistry.

In nurseries and primary classrooms all children are offered opportunities to work with a wide variety of materials, tools and equipment. For example, girls and boys will use construction kits to design and make models; girls and boys will study food technology, so that they learn about food, what they should eat to help them to grow and to be healthy, and both will learn some cookery techniques. Sometimes children have acquired the attitudes of older generations, who may still believe that 'boys will be boys and girls will be girls'. In order to encourage all children to take part in the activities some nurseries and schools carry out an audit of children's chosen activities.

Gender bias can also be shown, usually subconsciously, by the adults working with the children. The following are some typical examples of subconscious gender bias and are to be avoided:
- lining up: girls first then the boys;
- referring to the children by their gender, for example, 'All the boys can go out to play now';
- grouping children by gender: boys working with boys and girls with girls.

Activity 2.4 Observation checklist Complete the record on Activity sheet 2 for the children that you work with. This will help you to identify any bias in the children's choice of activity.

Discussion The traditional bias occurs where children are given free choice. You may have found that the boys preferred construction activities and playing with garages and cars, whilst the girls chose quieter activities. This is not always so, however, and all children should be encouraged to try all types of activity. Check that the instructions you give to children do not show gender bias, and that children are encouraged to work in mixed gender groups, where that is appropriate.

Notes to leaders

- Ask each of the assistants to 'draw a scientist'. Do they produce a stereotypical man in a white coat as their scientist? Discuss the implications of this view of 'what a scientist is' for their own role in school.
- Provide a number of educational catalogues for the assistants to find out more about the equipment available for science and design and technology activities.
- Encourage the assistants to ask their teachers about the problems that can occur when storing and accessing science and design and technology equipment in the school. What methods do each of the schools have for keeping track of the equipment?

Supporting understanding

Further reading

The Design and Technology Association (1996) *Primary Design and Technology. A Guide for Teacher Assistants*. Wellesbourne: DATA.

Dunne, D. (ed.) (1996) *The New Sc1Book*. Northampton: Northamptonshire Inspection and Advisory Service.

Harlen, W. (ed.) (1985) *Primary Science: Taking the Plunge*. London: Heinemann Educational.

Harlen, W. (1996) *The Teaching of Science in Primary Schools*, 2nd ed. London: David Fulton Publishers.

CHAPTER 3

Health and safety

This chapter explores considerations of health and safety in science and design and technology. The specific issues discussed include:
- safety in the classroom;
- using equipment;
- testing designs;
- using household 'chemicals' and substances;
- heating and burning;
- electricity;
- using food;
- living things;
- working outside.

Young children are not aware of the dangers around them. They will run out into the road, unless prevented, because they have no sense of the danger which traffic presents. Similarly they will pull at objects which they want to examine, sometimes causing themselves serious burns and scalds. As children grow older, they gradually become aware of the hazards around them and will take precautions to prevent themselves from being hurt. By the time they reach adulthood they will identify most dangers and take preventative measures to avoid being injured.

Risk assessment

Most children have natural curiosity and want to explore their environment. In school this curiosity is to be encouraged, but at the same time children must not be placed in dangerous or harmful situations. In the classroom it is the responsibility of the adults to ensure that children are safe. This is done through identifying **hazards** and calculating the **risk** of harm:
- **Hazard:** something that could cause harm. Obvious examples include electricity and boiling water; far from obvious would be high levels of lead in paint, or a picture hanging from a nail.
- **Risk:** this is identified through taking account of the seriousness of the harm caused by the hazard together with the likelihood of the harm actually happening. Sometimes risk is expressed as a formula: degree of severity × likelihood.

In order to ensure the children's safety it is important to undertake risk assessment within and outside the classroom.

Activity 3.1 Risk assessment in the home At home, identify some hazards and decide what level of risk these present. Use Activity sheet 3 to record your findings.

Working with children Before beginning any activity with children check that the environment is free from high risk. If there is a hazard that is medium risk, discuss this with the teacher to agree what safety measures should be taken. Children should be encouraged to take increasing responsibility for themselves and to begin to identify possible hazards. As they prepare for an activity discuss safety issues with them, such as looking where they walk when carrying a box of equipment in order to avoid tripping.

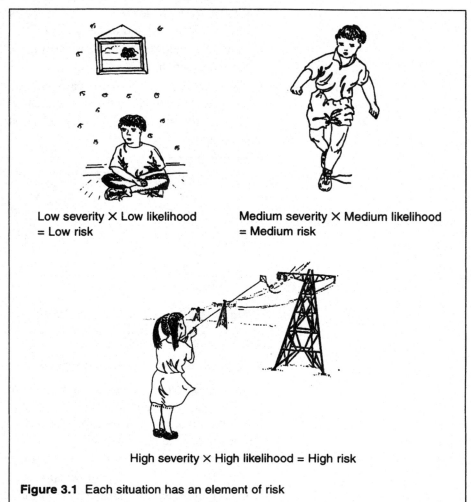

Low severity × Low likelihood = Low risk

Medium severity × Medium likelihood = Medium risk

High severity × High likelihood = High risk

Figure 3.1 Each situation has an element of risk

First aid

There will be someone responsible for first aid and a place where first aid materials are to be found at school. All adults must be aware of how first aid help can be found and of the school's health and safety policy. Sometimes there are accidents with equipment, which will need to be cleared away. Find out where cleaning materials are kept, such as gloves, cloths, dustpans and brushes, buckets and mops.

Using equipment

Science and design and technology activities frequently require children to use equipment and how to use this safely is a prime concern of the adult working with the children.

Safety measures when using tools

Children must be supervised whilst using tools. Be certain, before you begin the activity, that *you* know how to use the tools safely. Always check that the children know how to use the tools.

- Scissors: there are various types of scissors available, some of which are particularly suitable for younger children.
- Craft knives: these are not suitable for use with younger children and their use should be limited to the adult in the classroom.
- Saws: the material to be sawn should be firmly attached with a clamp to the work bench.
- Hammers: ones with small heads should be used. These are lighter and less likely to cause serious damage if a child hammers her finger.
- Hand drills: the material to be drilled should be fixed in a vice to avoid slipping.

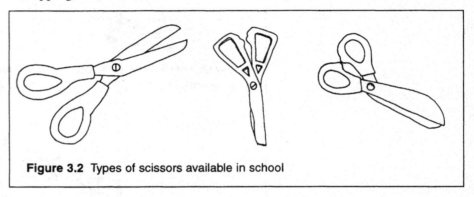

Figure 3.2 Types of scissors available in school

Safety measures when using glues

There are various types of glue available for use in school and the correct one for the purpose must be used. 'Super glue' and wallpaper pastes with fungicide must not be used. The following are safety considerations to take into account when using glue.

- Younger children should wear an apron or overall before using glue as it can be very difficult to remove spills from clothing.
- Cool melt glue guns are much safer than hot glue guns and should only be used with adult supervision and not at all with pre-fives.
- Glues with a strong odour should not be used.
- The working surface should be protected from the glue with a plasticised cloth or with newspaper.

Using materials which may break

Cooking vessels such as Pyrex or pottery bowls will break if dropped. Glass thermometers and mirrors will also break if dropped and schools will usually have plastic mirrors and safer, non-glass thermometers. Encourage the children to take care when using breakable materials. Plastic mirrors are much safer than glass ones and give reasonable quality reflections. If a young child breaks something that is made from glass or pottery, an adult should clean up.

Safe storage

Tools must be stored safely in a specially designed box or hanging from a board. Scissors may be stored in a special scissors rack. As they work remind the children to keep their work area tidy. When they have finished an activity encourage them to put the tools away themselves, so that they begin to take some responsibility for safety. Similarly glass and ceramic items should be stored safely.

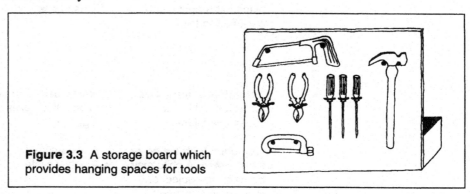

Figure 3.3 A storage board which provides hanging spaces for tools

Choosing appropriate tools

Encourage children to choose the appropriate tool for the task by discussing with them what they want to achieve.

Activity 3.2 Tool chest search Look at the tools available in school. Check that you know how to use each one. Decide on risks associated with using the tools and how you would ensure that children are safe.

Working with children The children's safety when using tools and equipment is your concern. Always make sure that you have assessed the likely risks and ensured that the working environment is as safe as possible. Always show them the correct way to hold and use a tool when they meet it for the first time and check as they work that they are following these procedures. Do encourage the children to consider their and each other's safety as they work. They can be encouraged to help to prepare an activity, thinking about the materials and tools that they will use and how to carry them safely. Do remember to ensure that children's clothing is protected if there is risk of damage.

There will probably be some left-handed children in the class. They will benefit from using tools designed for left-handed use. Left-handed scissors are readily available, and so too are tape measures made especially for left-handed use. Where left-handed children have to use right-handed tools, they will have difficulty in holding the tools in a comfortable position and, for measuring tapes, will find making accurate measurement difficult as the tape will be back to front from their view point.

Testing designs

Children will design and make models and structures, sometimes to produce a finished product, at other times to carry out an experiment.

Risks and safety factors

Check the risks and how to minimise them before children test their model or structure (see Table 3.1).

Table 3.1 Ensuring that risks have been minimised to a safe level before the activity begins

Risk	Example of activity	Safety measures
Objects which may fall. This may be an accidental fall or something which is placed at a height and designed to fall.	• Testing the breaking point of cotton thread. • Making a structure from newspaper to support a house brick.	• Children take care to keep out of the way when an object is dropped. • Put a box with soft or waste material in it under the object designed to fall so that landing is cushioned.
Snapping of stretched materials. This can cause eye injuries.	• Elastic bands stretched to hold two boxes together.	• Consider whether goggles should be worn.
Objects which swing or hang down. A child may be hit by the object or it may come loose and cause an injury.	• A pendulum. • A pulley system.	• Ensure that there is adequate space for the swing. • Ask children to stand clear. • Ensure that hanging objects and pulley systems are securely fixed.
Large constructions where children will sit inside or on top.	• Models made with Quadro or similar construction kits.	• Check that the construction is secure and strong before it is used.

Safety measures when testing things that fly

Children love making flying objects, such as kites, hot-air balloons and gliders. These can be hazardous if misused. There are some simple rules to follow, which help to ensure safety.

- Fill hot-air balloons using a hair dryer – these can be flown indoors or outdoors.
- Never fly any object near power cables or an electricity sub-station.
- Launch parachutes and boomerangs into a clear space – always take especial care if children are going to drop a parachute from an up-stairs window or stairwell.
- Catapults must be used with care – choose safe projectiles such as ping pong balls and launch away from spectators.

Activity 3.3 Kites away! Make and test the kite in Figure 3.4. Assess the risks before you start and decide upon the measures to adopt to ensure your safety.

Working with children If there is time, try out an activity yourself before you supervise the children at work. This approach will enable you to be more certain that you have identified and covered all the possible risks. Try the kite making activity with a group of children. You should feel confident that they will be safe.

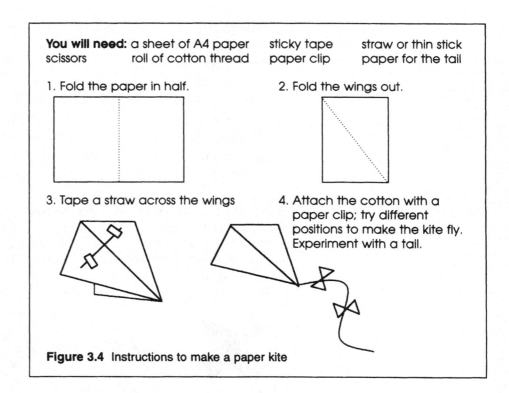

Figure 3.4 Instructions to make a paper kite

Using chemicals

Risks

Many ordinary household substances will be used in science experiments with nursery- and primary-aged children. These substances include, for example, aluminium foil, hand-washing detergent, soap and lemon juice. Young children will attempt to put these things into their mouths, and so whatever is used must be safe if they should try to taste it.

Safety measures when using household substances

There are some simple rules that will help to minimise the risks. Young children will not be using dangerous substances, but should still begin to understand the routines for ensuring safety when using chemicals.

- Use spoons for removing solid substances such as baking powder or bath salts from storage containers, never fingers.
- Use droppers for transferring liquids into a container.
- Only use small quantities at a time. This will prevent the need to pour any surplus back into its storage container, avoiding contamination and spillage.
- Prevent contact with eyes. This can happen if a chemical 'spits' when it is being heated. Consider whether children should wear goggles.
- Avoid skin contact with chemicals and consider whether children should use disposable gloves, especially if they are known to have sensitive skin.
- Always wipe up spills at once, taking care to protect the hands.
- Always wash hands after using chemicals.

Safety measures when storing chemicals

- Store chemicals in clearly labelled containers. For items such as baking powder or lemon juice, this can be their original container.
- Avoid transferring chemicals into empty food or drink containers. The use

of these could confuse children who might think that these chemicals are safe to eat or drink.
- Keep small quantities of the chemicals to ensure that they are as fresh as possible and to avoid deterioration.
- Store the chemicals in a safe, locked cupboard, away from food storage and heat sources. This will help children to understand that these chemicals are for use in experiments, and not to be eaten or drunk.
- Refer to the school's health and safety policy for specific instructions on storage.

Activity 3.4 Dangerous substances Look carefully at the labels on these containers: detergent, lavatory cleaner, oven cleaner, bleach, nail varnish remover and gloss paint. What are the hazards? How should they be stored? *Are any of these safe to use with young children? Which safety symbols are used on the packaging?*

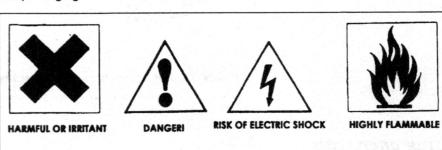

Figure 3.5 Always ensure that you read the labels on substances to check for hazards before using them with children

Working with children Some household substances are very dangerous indeed. Some, such as oven cleaner and lavatory cleaner, are corrosive, and if swallowed will cause serious internal injuries. These chemicals will be available in school for cleaning purposes and must be stored securely, away from children's reach. Make sure that children are aware of the safety measures to be employed as they work with household substances, and the reasons for this. As they enter Year 4, they should be becoming aware of other dangers and begin to recognise and respect the international warning symbols used on some, but not all, containers of hazardous chemicals. Children must be aware that it is not safe to experiment by mixing substances together at home.

Heating and burning

Risks

Children will, from time to time, use hot water or a candle flame to heat a substance. This can be hazardous. If the water is too hot there are risks of scalding and candle flames can be the cause of fires.

Safety measures for heating and burning

If the following safety measures are always followed, the risk of injury or danger will be reduced. However, vigilance, on both the children's and adult's part, is always needed in order to avoid accidents.
- There must be close adult supervision. Tie back long hair. Have cold water available in case of burns or scalds.
- Explain that hot water and steam can scald and that items held over a candle flame will be very hot and will burn if they are touched.
- Provide goggles to protect the eyes when heating chemicals.

- Use candles and night lights in metal sand trays so that they are firmly sited and burning fragments are caught in the sand; or put night lights in commercial candle holders for stability. Dispose of matches carefully.
- When heating use a small sample of the substance to avoid spillages.
- Where hot water is required, use water from the hot tap.
- Where an oven or boiling ring is used for heating, make sure that the saucepan handles face inwards to avoid accidental knocks and spills. Switch off immediately after use.
- Glass thermometers will break if dropped. Dial thermometers, such as a Thermostik, are much safer but less sensitive to changes in temperature. Do not use a mercury-filled thermometer, as these are dangerous if broken.

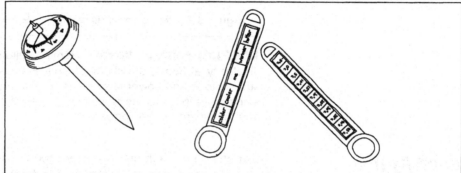

Figure 3.6 There are many different types of thermometer available for use in school, including the Thermostik and simple thermometers with liquid crystal displays

Activity 3.5 Heating Make a spoon shape from aluminium foil. Attach it to a wooden clothes peg. Fix a nightlight firmly in a metal tray with sand in it. Now use the spoon to heat some sugar. What are the hazards? How would you ensure that the risk was reduced to a low level?

Working with children Substances can be heated in metal spoons, or in spoon shapes made from aluminium foil if held with a wooden clothes peg. Spoons must be placed on a safe surface after heating. Long hair should be tied back and loose clothing fixed so that nothing trails over the candle flame. Children will need very careful supervision whilst heating substances in this way. Make them aware of the dangers, but do not frighten them! Ask them to explain why such care is taken when heating substances over a naked flame.

Using electricity

Children will not use mains electricity for science or design and technology at school other than for plug-in apparatus such as computers, and these will be set up by an adult.

Risks

Where mains equipment is in use, there are high levels of risk if it is not maintained correctly. All electrical appliances in school must be checked annually by a qualified electrician and test labelled. Never use equipment that has a damaged plug or frayed lead. Children will use batteries for electricity. As long as the voltage of these is low, preferably 1.5 volts to 9 volts it is not possible to get an electric shock unless a large number of these batteries are wired together. Rechargeable batteries should not be used except inside other equipment such as torches, tape recorders and motors for driving models and constructions. This is to avoid a risk of short circuiting, which causes the batteries and wires to get very hot and can cause a burn if touched.

Safety measures with electricity

- Store batteries so that the terminals do not touch, to avoid short-circuiting.
- Dispose of old batteries, as there is a danger of them leaking.
- Never cut open old batteries as the contents are dangerous.
- Ensure that the correct type of charging unit for rechargeable batteries is used.

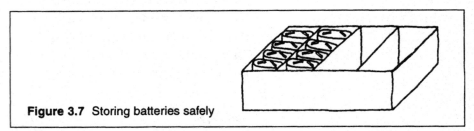

Figure 3.7 Storing batteries safely

Working with children Remind children of the dangers associated with electricity at home, at school and outside, such as the dangers that electricity sub-stations and power lines present. Also remind them of the good things that electricity does, such as providing sources of warmth and cooking, entertainment and the power for the computer.

Food hygiene

Children enjoy helping to prepare food. Cooking activities are an important element of science and design and technology.

Risks

Children put their hands in their mouths as they work, and they often forget to wash their hands after visiting the lavatory or cover their mouth if they cough or sneeze. All of these actions can spread bacteria, which will lead to infected food.

Safety measures when working with food

Ensure that children follow normal hygiene measures before and during handling food.

- Tie back long hair.
- Wash hands thoroughly with soap and water.
- Wear aprons kept especially for cooking.
- Cover cuts and scratches with waterproof dressings.
- Be especially careful to avoid foods containing or contaminated with nuts as some children can be extremely allergic to nuts.
- Use equipment that is kept just for work with food.
- Ensure that all surfaces and utensils are thoroughly clean.
- Ensure that an adult places food to be cooked in the oven.
- Store raw and cooked foods correctly, refrigerating where necessary.
- Wrap unwanted foods before disposing of them carefully.

Activity 3.6 Handling food safely Visit your local supermarket and observe the safety measures that the staff take to ensure that fresh food remains safe. How does this differ from your own practice in the kitchen?

Working with children At home we may be slap-dash in our approach to food preparation, but at school it is essential that risks of contamination, spread of disease and of burns and scalds are kept to a minimum. When working with children it may well be necessary to remind them every time they visit the lavatory, even during the activity, that they must wash their hands.

Living things

Living things includes the study of ourselves, animals, micro-organisms and plants. Many children will have their own pets at home, and so have some awareness of the safety factors involved in caring for animals. Others may be keen collectors and pick up dead animals and feathers, thus risking the spread of disease.

'Ourselves'

This is a very popular topic at nursery and in school. Children enjoy finding out about themselves and how their bodies work.

Risks

There may be children in the group who for health reasons have to avoid strenuous exercise and should not be asked to undertake strenuous exercise in scientific experiments. Avoid making direct comparisons between children so that nobody considers themselves abnormal.

Safety measures with ourselves

- Be aware of any health issues amongst the children, such as asthma, epilepsy or eczema, and of any special precautions that must be taken.
- Where foods are used for an investigation, ensure that surfaces and utensils are clean.
- Wash hands before handling foods.
- Use disposable items where things are to be put into the mouth.
- Do not take blood samples as there is a risk of infection from this.
- Avoid listening to loud sounds as prolonged exposure to loud noise can damage hearing.
- Do not allow children to look directly at the sun or other sources of bright light.

Animals

In some classrooms animals such as goldfish or hamsters will be kept. There may also be garden creatures, such as worms or frogspawn, which are being studied. It is better to avoid animals in the classroom as they can find classroom living very stressful.

Risks

Some children may be allergic to animals, especially furry ones. Birds must not be kept in the classroom because of the risk of spreading disease.

Safety measures with animals

- Always wash hands before and after handling animals.
- Consult a reputable book on the care of animals in the classroom.
- Keep the housing clean.
- Where animals are placed on tables or the floor, ensure that the surfaces are thoroughly cleaned immediately afterwards.

- Handle animals with care; bites and scratches must be washed immediately and an anti-tetanus injection will be required.
- Never bring dead or live wild animals such as birds, hedgehogs or mice into the classroom as these may spread disease.

Activity 3.7 Animal care Find a reputable book or RSPCA guidelines about an animal kept at school. Plan a timetable for its care during the week and for the weekend. Note possible hazards and safety measures to be taken.

Working with children Children probably do not take special precautions at home when playing with their pets. At school the safety measures must be followed to ensure that children, and the animals, are safe. What arrangements have been made for caring for the animals during the weekend or school holidays? Some homes will offer good care, while others will have good intentions but not be aware of the level of commitment that caring for animals involves.

Micro-organisms

These include yeasts and moulds.

Risks

These should be minimal in the primary school, as activities will involve safe observation, rather than growing yeasts and moulds.

Safety measures with micro-organisms

- Tell the children that they must not put anything in their mouths when handling any containers with micro-organisms.
- Cover cuts and scratches with a waterproof dressing.
- Wash hands after handling the containers.
- Keep moulds in a transparent container with a tight fitting lid which must not be removed.
- Put a plug of cotton wool in the top of the glass jar in which yeasts are kept. This will allow the carbon dioxide which the yeast produces to escape safely into the atmosphere.
- Observe changes in the micro-organisms without uncovering them.
- Wipe up any spills immediately using disinfectant and disposable gloves.
- Dispose of the container and micro-organisms if it smells or when the investigation has finished, following the school policy for disposal.

Plants

Many schools have gardens so that children can observe plants growing.

Risks

Some plants or part of plants may be poisonous if eaten, or cause a rash if touched. Some children may be especially sensitive to particular plants.

Safety measures with plants

- Check that the seeds or plants are not poisonous and that they are safe to touch.
- Avoid touching the eyes when handling plants.
- Never taste any part of a plant unless absolutely safe to do so.

- Never use seeds which have been coated with pesticides or fungicides.
- Always wash hands after handling plants and soil.

Activity 3.8 Medical alert   Find out which children have medical conditions which may affect their work with living things. This could include asthma and eczema, for example. Check on these children's medical needs. Do they need to take special precautions? Where are their inhalers stored and when should these be used?

Working with children   For children with medical conditions it is essential to know how to deal with an emergency should the need arise. Check with the class teacher what procedures are to be followed in the unlikely event of a child suffering an asthma or epilepsy attack. You may be the only adult there and must know what to do. Remember to reassure all the children, not just the one who is ill.

Working outside

Investigations and problem-solving activities will take children outside the classroom, perhaps into the playground or the school's garden or nature reserve.

Risks

There are dangers outside which young children especially will not recognise, such as ponds full of water and the risk of falling over and cutting themselves. Cuts can become infected, possibly with tetanus.

Safety measures when working outside

- Even on cloudy days, ensure that children are protected from the harmful rays of the sun and consider whether they need to wear long sleeves and sun hats and use sun block.
- Wear suitable clothing and footwear.
- Cover cuts and scratches with waterproof dressings to avoid the risk of infection.
- Check the outside area for any hazards, such as broken glass.
- Visits to the pond must always be accompanied by adults. Do not leave children unattended.
- Use plastic spoons or soft paintbrushes to collect minibeasts and insects.
- Put any feathers collected into sealed plastic bags.
- When gardening, ensure that children know how to use the tools safely. Children should only use garden tools when supervised by an adult.

Figure 3.8 Garden tools only to be used when supervised by an adult

- Never look directly at the sun in any circumstances.
- Do not leave lenses or magnifiers lying about as the sun's rays can be focused through the glass and cause a fire.
- If collecting litter, ensure that children wear disposable gloves to avoid infection or cuts, or use litter grabbers.

Activity 3.9 Risk assessment at school   Carry out a risk assessment of the outside area at school. Use Activity sheet 4 to record your observations.

Working with children   Children enjoy working outside in the fresh air. They will not be as aware of danger as adults are and so the adult accompanying them must be especially vigilant. Before working outside, always undertake a risk assessment and ensure that hazards are avoided.

Notes to leaders

☞ Encourage the assistants to identify hazards in their workplace and to assess the level of risk to the children and themselves.
☞ Ask the assistants to work in pairs and discuss how they might reduce the level of risk.
☞ In their notebooks the assistants can keep a log of hazards which they identify during the week and the actions they took in order to reduce the risk.

Supporting understanding

Ideas for working with children

IChemE and NIAS. *Health and Safety Activities Box*. Northampton: Northamptonshire County Council.
Child Accident Prevention Trust, *Keeping Kids Safe*. A book of activities and information. London: CAPT.
Health Education Authority's Primary School Project. '*Health for life*', curriculum materials and teachers' guide. London: HEA.
Royal Society for the Prevention of Accidents. Books, leaflets, posters, audio visual aids, activity packs and a wide range of teachers' guides. Birmingham: RSPA.

Further reading

Association for Science Education (1994) *Safety in Science for Primary Schools*. Hatfield: ASE.
Association for Science Education (1990) *Be Safe!* Hatfield: ASE.

CHAPTER 4
Working with children

This chapter considers how to help children to develop:
- their thinking about science and design and technology;
- their vocabulary, including specific scientific and technological language;
- their recording skills, including the use of Information Technology (IT).

Questioning techniques are considered in detail, in particular when and how to ask open, rather than closed, questions.

Finding out about children's ideas in science and design and technology

Many adults look back to the time that they were taught science and design and technology (or 'craft') at school as a time when they were required by their teacher to find the 'right' answer. Teacher had a particular answer in mind so children played a game of 'guess what teacher is thinking'. Today's teaching is very different from that, as children are encouraged to explore their own ideas, to design scientific investigations and technological models, to carry out their investigation, make their model and to evaluate the outcomes. Through this process children reconsider their original ideas and form concepts based upon their experiences. As they extend their experiences through further investigation so they develop their knowledge, skills and understanding of scientific facts and processes, and design and technological processes. For children to be successful scientists the adults with whom they work need to know about and understand the relevant science. For children to be successful technologists the adults with whom they work need to understand the processes and explain and demonstrate the relevant skills.

To find out about children's ideas it is important to make time for discussion. This discussion should be based upon ideas, phenomena and materials which are within the children's experience. For example, the task could be to find suitable materials for a raincoat to keep teddy dry. Children's own experiences are most valuable here, and they can be encouraged to discuss what they wear when it rains, and how effective it is at keeping them dry. They might discuss the times that they have been caught in a shower of rain, what they were wearing and how wet they became. This discussion is very important as it offers children the opportunity to discuss their experiences and to consider each other's ideas.

At each stage of the learning process, it is important to give children the opportunity to discuss their ideas. This gives the adult working with the children insights into what children are thinking and, through careful and sensitive questioning, further insights into their explanations of what they have observed and how they have interpreted this. Discussion is central to the 'plan, do and review' cycle, helping children to develop their ideas and understanding (see Figure 4.1).

As children talk about their ideas in science and design and technology the adult should encourage them to make predictions of what they think will happen if a particular action is taken. For example, when discussing which

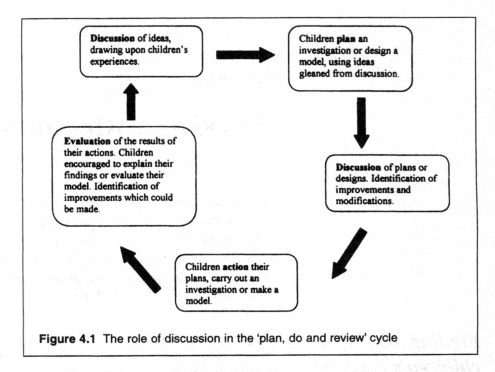

Figure 4.1 The role of discussion in the 'plan, do and review' cycle

materials to test to find suitable fabrics for teddy's raincoat, children might predict that cotton jersey (T-shirt fabric) would be a poor choice because their T-shirt was soaked after being out in the rain. They might also predict that plastic would be a good choice because they brought a goldfish home from the shop in a plastic bag with water inside and the water did not leak out. On the other hand, another child might predict that woollen material would be a good choice because her winter coat kept her warm. In this example, the child may associate warmth with dryness, and may not have experienced what happens to her woollen coat when it gets wet. All of these predictions can be tested by carrying out an investigation.

Activity 4.1 Children's ideas Ask the teacher if you may make a tape recording of the children's discussion. Work with a small group of children in a quiet place and explain that you would like to record their discussion. Explain what the task will be: a scientific investigation or a design and technology task. Now ask the children for their ideas about how to carry out the task and what they think will happen. As soon after the lesson as you can, listen to the tape and write down the children's ideas. Write down your observations about their ideas.

Discussion Children's own ideas may be scientifically valid or technologically sound. On the other hand, they may put forward ideas, based on their experiences, which are different from the accepted scientific view. They may have misunderstandings about the technological properties of materials and how these can be used to make models and structures.

It is not appropriate to say to children 'No, that is wrong'. Their existing ideas can be used as a starting point for developing their learning. It is the responsibility of the adult to help them to construct an investigation or rethink their design for a model so that they can test their ideas and, through discussion of their experiences and consideration of the evidence that they gather, to help them to reconstruct their ideas so that they understand the scientific and technological principles involved.

Research into the existing ideas of children in relation to science

There have been a number of studies in the last 20 years into the existing ideas that children may hold in relation to their knowledge and understanding of science. The work which is most relevant to primary children has been carried out by the Science Processes and Concepts Exploration (SPACE), a joint project based at Liverpool University and King's College, London. They produced research reports (1990–1992) on growth and light, amongst others, and more recently they have worked with the Nuffield Foundation to produce the Nuffield Primary Science scheme (1995) in which the existing ideas that children may hold are discussed and used as a basis for further work. These publications give detailed insights into children's ideas about science.

Vocabulary for science and design and technology

Science

Children are expected to learn the 'scientific' vocabulary to name and describe living things, materials, phenomena and processes for the work in 'Life processes and living things', 'Materials and their properties' and 'Physical processes'. Many of the words used will have an everyday meaning, and may be confusing to the children unless the adults working with them have a clear understanding of the scientific meaning of the word. To gain this understanding, the adults need to have a good working knowledge of the specific area, and the relevant vocabulary is discussed in Chapters 5, 6 and 7 of this book. For example, the meaning of 'animal' is discussed in Chapter 5: the word 'animal' is often used by adults as well as children to describe a cuddly creature such as a cat or a dog but not an earthworm. Children need to discuss this with an adult who has a good understanding of the breadth of the animal kingdom so that they gain a much clearer definition of the term 'animal'.

In 'Experimental and investigative science', there are terms used that have a particular meaning in a scientific context. As already discussed in Chapter 3 the starting point for practical work may be from a number of different sources and the children may be focussing on one or more areas of the process skills in a session. In planning experimental work children need:

- new vocabulary from the subject area that will enable them to express their ideas, including the names of equipment that might be used. For example, if they were planning an investigation involving growing seeds, the vocabulary might include: seed, soil, pot, water, light, dark, height, measure.
- the vocabulary to talk about what might happen if they try out their ideas. If they have previous experience of the area that they are studying, they may be able to predict what will happen – a prediction is not a 'guess'; it should be based on past evidence. If the work is totally new to the children, predicting an outcome may be very difficult.
- the vocabulary to help them put their ideas into a suitable form for investigating. The children may be investigating the effect of water on the growth of seeds. They may think that water is needed for seeds to grow and so their idea may be 'we are going to find out if seeds need water to grow'. They will then think about how they would do this.
- the vocabulary and the concept of variables to gain an understanding of the idea of 'fair testing'. The variables are the things that can change in an investigation. Fair testing involves controlling these variables so that children consider one at a time. In the investigation to find out if seeds need water to grow, two identical pots of seeds would be set up and left in the same conditions, except that one pot would be watered and the other left dry.

In obtaining evidence children need:
- the appropriate vocabulary to talk about the ways in which they use their senses to explore materials and objects. This work is discussed in the relevant sections of Chapters 5 and 6 of this book.
- the appropriate vocabulary for the pieces of equipment that they use for close observation, such as hand lenses, and the equipment used for measuring. There will need to be close links here with their work in mathematics as they consider how and what to measure.
- new vocabulary when making observations and measurements of their findings. If they have grown bean seeds, they would need to use the correct terms for the parts of the bean plant and be able to name suitable equipment for measuring the growth.

In considering evidence children need:
- the vocabulary to enable them to talk to others about their work and to explain what they have found out.
- the vocabulary to talk about their drawings, tables and charts to present their results to others. This may involve looking for patterns to show what happened.
- the vocabulary to discuss whether their evidence supports any predictions they made and to draw conclusions about the results. They will need to refer to their original statement and check that they have investigated what they set out to look at, such as whether they have found out if seeds need water to grow.

Design and technology

Children are expected to learn the appropriate vocabulary for naming and describing the equipment, materials and components they use. Such vocabulary includes the names of the tools that they use, the various types of materials that they may choose, including plastic, card, paper, wood, fabrics and threads and malleables such as plasticine, as well as the vocabulary of parts from construction kits, including gears, pulleys, axles and wheels. They will also need to understand the specific language used in describing the process of designing, making and evaluating.

Designing refers to the process of:
- deciding what needs to be done;
- thinking and talking through ideas of how to proceed;
- planning what is to be done, the materials and tools to be used, and how to fasten the components together;
- developing the ideas through producing a picture, diagram, or exploring how materials can be used;
- evaluating designs to identify strengths and to improve on weaknesses.

Young children will often combine the process of designing and making by exploring what the materials can do and developing their ideas as they work.

Adults need to understand the process implicit in 'designing' and to encourage children to use the vocabulary of the design process and the materials and tools which they may wish to use in their discussions.

Making refers to the process of:
- working with materials and tools to measure, mark out, cut, shape, join and finish their model;

- planning ahead to anticipate what needs to be done first, and how to carry this out.

Adults should encourage children to think through the process of making and to decide upon a suitable order of events. As children work, they should use the language associated with measuring as they measure and cut out materials. This offers good opportunities to use the language of mathematics and, in particular, numbers in the context of measuring.

Evaluating is the process of:
- considering finished work and commenting upon its effectiveness;
- making decisions about possible improvements;
- identifying the strengths of a design;
- considering the efficiency of the whole process of designing and making and identifying other possible solutions.

Through the process of evaluation adults should encourage children to think about what they have done by asking questions such as:
- 'Does this work well?'
- 'What would improve it?'
- 'What other materials could we have chosen?'
- 'How would these have improved the design/model?'

Developing questioning skills

There are two types of questions:
- **open questions**, where there is no 'right' answer and where children can respond with their own ideas and understanding. An example is 'What do you think would happen if ...?' This question can be used in both scientific and technological discussion to encourage children to make predictions, use their experiences to think about what might happen, and to draw upon their existing knowledge and understanding.
- **closed questions**, where there is just one answer. These are very useful where a specific response is needed, but should not be used when children are being encouraged to think and reflect upon the task in hand. Closed questions are used to determine whether:
  - a child has learnt specific vocabulary: 'Tell me the name of this';
  - a child has been listening to what has been said: 'How do we do this?';
  - and to explain how to use a tool safely: 'Tell me how to hold/use this.'

Using open questions in science

Children's understanding in all areas of science can be explored by using open questions:
- 'What can you tell me about ...?'
- 'What do you know about ...?'
- 'What do you think this is?'
- 'What do you think this could be used for?'

Questions can become more focused and still be open. A teacher might show children an earthworm and ask the question 'What can you tell me about this creature?' If nobody mentions movement she may then ask the children to focus on the way the earthworm moves by asking 'How does it move?' Young children may use their own bodies to show how the worm moves and their teacher can help them with the vocabulary needed to describe the movements.

Open questioning by an adult will support children in sorting out their own ideas in relation to practical activities, and as they become more experienced they will be able to use this type of questioning to work more independently. Use the following questions for scientific investigations.

Planning experimental work
- 'What are you going to try to find out?'
- 'What are you going to do?'
- 'What do you think will happen?'
- 'How will you do it?'
- 'What equipment will you need?'
- 'What will you change?'
- 'What will you keep the same to make sure this test is fair?'
- 'How will you make sure this work is safe?'

Obtaining evidence
- 'What will you measure?'
- 'What are you looking for?'
- 'How will you record what you measure?'
- 'How will you record what you see happening?'

Considering evidence
- 'How will you present and share your results to others?'
- 'What do your results tell you?'
- 'How do your results compare with what you thought would happen?'
- 'What have you found out by doing this work?'
- 'What made your test fair?'
- 'How could you improve on what you did?'

Using open questions in design and technology

The design and technology process lends itself to the asking of open questions. Use the following suggestions for open questions during the planning process so that you have some starter questions to help you to ask open questions in the context in which the children are working.

Designing
- 'Who might use it?'
- 'What size will it need to be?'
- 'What materials might you use?'
- 'How are you going to fix it together?'
- 'How does it work?'
- 'What would happen if ...?'
- 'Which do you prefer?'

Making
- 'What will you do first? Why?'
- 'What materials will you need?'
- 'What tools will you need?'
- 'What would be the best way to ...?'
- 'How can you make that the right size?'
- 'How could you make it stronger?'
- 'How could you make it look better?'

Evaluating
- 'What does it do?'
- 'How does it work?'
- 'What would make it better?'
- 'What is good about this model?'

Activity 4.2 Asking questions Prepare some open questions to ask the children during a science or design and technology activity. Try the questions with the children and, with the class teacher's permission, record the session so that you can listen to and analyse the responses from the children after the session has finished.

Discussion It is always helpful to prepare open questions before you begin so that you are clear about what you need to ask to generate discussion. If the children are not used to being asked this type of question, they may need some prompting to obtain answers. The purpose of this type of question is to encourage them to think things through for themselves. Try recording another activity at a later stage. You can then see how much their thinking skills have developed and also how much more confident you are at asking open questions.

Using language to promote scientific and technological thinking

Through the use of open questions children become more confident in expressing their ideas. It is important for the adult to accept individual ideas, even if these are 'wrong', and to help the child to develop their understanding through scientific investigation and through the designing, making and evaluating process. When this is used effectively, children feel safe to accept that previous ideas were misconceived and to rethink their ideas based upon their understanding of the outcomes of their work. Encouraging children to talk about their thinking at each stage of an investigation or design and make process helps them to develop their understanding of the ideas and concepts involved.

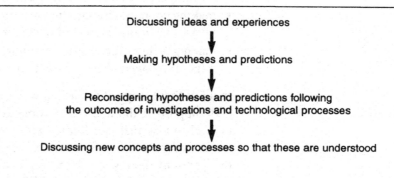

Figure 4.2 Encouraging children to talk about their thinking at each stage of an investigation or design and make process

When talking with children do take note of the following suggestions.
- Keep the discussion to the point: children may well want to talk about what happened at playtime, which would detract from the scientific or technological ideas being explored.
- Involve all the children, not just those who dominate the group. Encourage the quieter children with questions such as 'What do you think?' or 'What happened in your investigation?'.
- Listen to the children: they will give you valuable information about what they think and how they plan to work. This will help you to focus your discussion on specific needs.

- There are times when it is appropriate not to talk, for example, if a child is totally engrossed in a task and talking would be distracting, or if children are engaged in solving a problem and are likely to be successful. Talk with them later on, when they can explain how they solved the difficulty.
- Use an enthusiastic tone of voice, try to maintain eye contact with individuals in the group, and show by your body language that you are interested in them and what they have to say. This will help the children to feel valued and encourage them to discuss their work with you.
- Be aware of the scientific and technological vocabulary. Use this appropriately so that children hear the language forms and can practise using them themselves.
- While the children are working, you may observe that someone has found a useful solution to a problem. Decide whether to interrupt the work to ask the child to explain this to the others. Encourage the others to ask questions, and to show their appreciation of an interesting piece of work.

Recording outcomes of the work

There are many different ways in which the children can record what they have achieved. These include:
- producing a written report, to explain the process and to identify the findings. This could be a word-processed report.
- producing pictures to show what has occurred. These might be produced using a draw or paint software package on a computer.
- producing graphs to show results, perhaps using graphing software on the computer.
- using a simple spreadsheet to display results of an investigation.
- making a display of the products of a design and make project.
- making a display of the equipment children used in a scientific investigation, including their written results.
- making a photographic record of the sequence of events during an investigation or design and make project.
- making a tape recording of children's discussion of their work, which might be played to their parents or carers during a parents' evening.

In all of these ways of recording work, the children will benefit from the help and support of the adult. For some activities the recording will be agreed beforehand, so that the children know what will be expected of them towards the end of the activity. Sometimes children will be given a free choice of how they present their work. Here the adult will need to take into account the range of materials which should be readily available so that children can complete their recording.

Writing

Children can be asked to make written records to describe both what they intend to do – their planning – and the outcomes of the activity. A pre-determined format for planning helps them to focus on the process invoved.

Make sure that children have access to the materials that they need, including paper or exercise books and pencils or pens. Some children will need support with written work, including help with spelling difficult words. It can help to write new vocabulary which the children are to use on the board, flip chart or on a large sheet of paper to be placed on the table where they will work. Other children will want to use a dictionary to look up

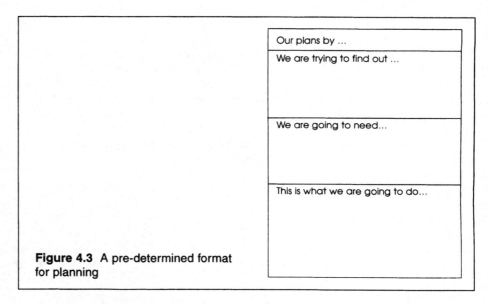

Figure 4.3 A pre-determined format for planning

difficult words. Ask the class teacher for guidance before the lesson begins on what help you should provide. Before the children begin, ask them what they intend to write and help them to organise their thoughts, in event order, so that they are clear about what they will record.

Pictures and diagrams

Provide suitable drawing and writing materials within easy reach of the children so that they can choose what they wish to use. Encourage them to discuss the drawings or diagrams that they intend to make, and to perhaps make a brief sketch on another piece of paper so that they have thought about the design and structure of what they intend to produce. Discuss with them the purpose of their drawing or diagram and ask them to explain its function and how it works.

Graphs

If children need to produce graphs to show their results, check that they have considered the type and scale of their graph. Younger children may stick items on to a sheet of paper to make a graph, such as lengths of string measured against them to show their height, and they may show one square to represent one object. Older children may use a scale, perhaps where one square represents two, five or ten objects. Discuss their finished graphs with them and ask them to read and interpret their own and each other's graphs, so helping them to use their mathematical knowledge in realistic situations.

Using computer software

You will need to know how to operate the classroom computer. Make sure that you know which software package to use, how to use it and how to save and print children's work. There should be a teacher coordinator for information technology who will be able to advise you.

Most schools have software for word-processing, where children can type their work on to the computer screen. Schools often use a different package for Key Stage 1 children from the package they use for Key Stage 2 children, so do check which one is suitable for the children with whom you are working. Children may like to work in pairs for this, so that they agree between them what they wish to write.

> We put out some peanuts and bird seed every morning.
> Then we watched the bird table.
> We saw some sparrows, blue tits, greenfinches and chaffinches.
> We wrote down how many birds we saw.
>
> **Figure 4.4** Using a word-processing software package, children can produce a neat version of their work

Figure 4.5 Children benefit from discussing their work when using the computer

Your school will probably have an art package, which may be for painting or drawing. This can be very useful for children to record in pictures, especially when producing a design for a product, or when drawing a picture of the results of an investigation.

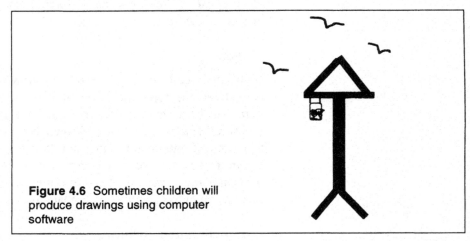

Figure 4.6 Sometimes children will produce drawings using computer software

For graphing, there are data packages which produce a range of different types of graph from the original data, including line and block graphs and pie charts. Discuss with your teacher before the lesson starts whether one type of graph would be most suitable, or whether the children should make that choice and then consider the suitability of their graphical representation.

Spreadsheets are useful for displaying results, especially where there is some arithmetic involved in obtaining the final result. Simple spreadsheets are usually used during Key Stage 2, rather than Key Stage 1, as the children should understand the arithmetical processes being used.

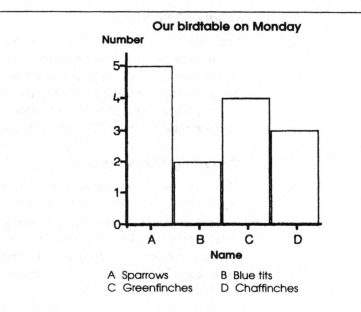

Figure 4.7 Children can input their data into a graphing software package and produce a neat, accurate graph

	Monday	Tuesday	Wednesday	Thursday	Friday
Sparrows	5	4	6	5	4
Blue tits	2	2	0	1	2
Greenfinches	4	3	2	0	4
Chaffinches	3	3	2	3	2
Total	14	12	10	9	12

Figure 4.8 Data from a topic can be entered into a spreadsheet software package

Making displays

Sometimes children will be asked to display their own work, perhaps by mounting writing or pictures on to larger sheets of paper; at other times they may display a finished product or model. Sometimes you will be asked to do this for them. Children's work on display must:

- represent that child's work worthy of praise. There is no point in displaying work that does not represent that child's best efforts, as that child and others will be aware that more could have been achieved. Displayed work should be representative of individuals' achievements.
- look attractive, so that the child who produced the work can feel pride in their achievement and know that others, children and adults, will also take pleasure from seeing it.
- be named. The child's name should be prominently displayed, so that they recognise the worth that their work has.
- be cared for. Displays should always be tidy, with torn lining paper repaired or replaced and items placed on top of a table kept neatly and tidily. This will help to ensure that the child takes pride in their own and other's work.
- be mentioned with pleasure by adults and other children. Encourage the children to say why they like an individual's work, so that each hears their own best work praised and praises that of others. This will help them to appreciate each other's strengths.

Taking photographs

Sometimes the most effective way to capture a child's achievement is by photographing what is happening. Classrooms or schools may have albums into which these photographs are placed to record achievement. At other times, photographs will be used as part of the display of a particular topic or project. These photographs are often taken by adults, but not always – children may occasionally take photographs of each other as a record.

Recording discussions

This can be a very useful way of recording children's achievements, especially for the shy child who can then listen to herself making valid discussion points. This is likely to boost her confidence and help her to feel comfortable in taking a greater part in group discussions. It can also be helpful for parents or carers to hear their child taking an active part in group work, especially where there has been concern about a child's performance in school.

Activity 4.3 Setting up a display Set up a display from which the children can use items to investigate or solve a problem. Decide with the class teacher on the focus of the display. When it is in use by some children, observe the way in which they use the display and listen to their discussion. What might you do to improve it further?

Discussion Interactive displays are a useful means of encouraging children to work independently of an adult. Sometimes they will so enjoy the problem or investigation that they will set another problem themselves for other children to enjoy. Such displays must be attractive to catch the children's attention and need to be regularly maintained, so that materials needed are renewed, and so that it is kept tidy to maintain its attraction.

Notes to leaders

- Encourage assistants to work in pairs, to ask open questions and to give each other feedback on their questioning skills.
- Using a science or design and technology focus, ask assistants to work in small groups to plan a wall display. Encourage them to consider its visual impact and how they would use children's work within the display.
- Provide opportunities for assistants to use commonly used word-processing, data handling and art software packages so that they become familiar with how these can be used to support learning.

Supporting understanding

Further reading

The Design and Technology Association (1996) *Primary Design and Technology: A Guide for Teacher Assistants.* Wellesbourne: DATA.

Fisher, J. (1996) *Starting from the Child.* Buckingham: Open University Press.

Harlen, W. (ed.) (1991) *Primary Science. Taking the Plunge.* Oxford: Heinemann Educational.

Harlen, W. (1996) *The Teaching of Science in Primary Schools,* 2nd ed. London: David Fulton Publishers.

Nuffield (1995) *Primary Science Teachers' Handbook.* London: Collins Educational.

SPACE (1992) *Reports of the SPACE Research Project.* Liverpool: Liverpool University Press.

CHAPTER 5

Life and living processes

This chapter considers the following key ideas:
- that children can be encouraged to explore and recognise the features of living things;
- that there are differences between living things and things that are not alive and how these characteristics (movement, growth, feeding, sensitivity, reproduction) are shown in animals and plants;
- that humans, as animals, need certain things in order to stay alive and healthy;
- that children can be guided to find out more about their own bodies and that there are similarities and differences between themselves and other pupils;
- that plants also need certain things to enable them to grow and produce seeds;
- that although there may be many different plants and animals in the local environment, these can be grouped by looking for certain features.

Children's early experiences

Children usually show a lively interest in their own bodies and those of other children because they have spent their first few years learning about what their bodies can do and how they can control many of their actions. New born babies are programmed to suckle soon after birth and to demand food from their carers by crying. At this stage babies do not realise that they are separate beings from their carers; this understanding develops during the first year as they start to focus upon their own hands and then use them to manipulate other objects. Babies' mouths are very sensitive and they will use this area to explore the shape and texture of objects, hence toys which can be held by a baby are usually taken into the mouth. Young children spend a large amount of time in learning how to feed themselves and later on most children find food an interesting topic to study. An equally time-consuming activity can result from parents' efforts to potty-train their child and discussion about what happens to food once the body has taken out the nutrients it needs; this often results in great hilarity amongst children.

Young children bring a wealth of knowledge with them about their own bodies, although they may not be able to express that knowledge because they do not know the recognised terms in the biological sense. Here adults need to be particularly sensitive to the language that the children might use.

Most children will also be fascinated by other animals, but their reactions may vary greatly from being very nervous to being dangerously over-confident when faced with, for example, a pet rabbit. They may only refer to small furry pets or farm or zoo animals when discussing the animal kingdom because they have not been encouraged to think of other creatures, such as spiders, as animals.

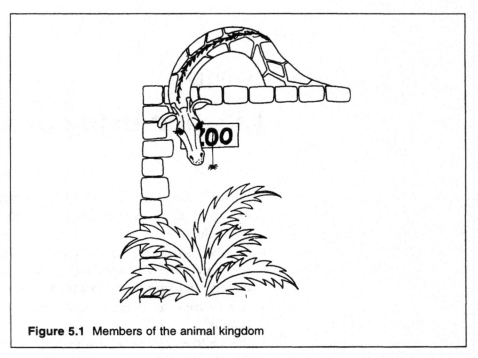

Figure 5.1 Members of the animal kingdom

Children do not generally find plants as interesting as animals because they do not move around, and although children will have seen plants in their surroundings they may not have noticed them.

Building key concepts

Life processes

Some of the characteristics of living things are that:
- they are able to move (most animals will move more quickly than plants);
- they can respond to changes in their surroundings by using their senses;
- they can get larger by growing;
- they can make new individuals by reproducing;
- they take in energy and materials from their surroundings for food and respiration.

If an organism does all of these things then it is alive. If it does not then it may never have been alive (like a metal spoon) or it may have been alive once but is no longer (like a wooden chair). It is not always easy to tell whether something is alive by just looking at it. Other information may be needed to make that decision. A handful of runner bean seeds may look very similar to a handful of pebbles, for example, but if the seeds are given water they will probably begin to grow.

Activity 5.1 Living or non-living? Look at the list on Activity sheet 5 and decide whether the items listed are:
- living;
- have never lived;
- were alive once.

Use the list of characteristics given earlier to help you decide.

Discussion Adults can use knowledge and understanding from previous experiences when deciding if things are alive or not. They need to know what things are made of before they can decide. A metal can has never been alive, while a cat is obviously alive even if it has not been allowed to have kittens. A feather was alive once when it was growing in the skin of a bird. As the feather grew away from the skin the blood supply stopped and so the cells forming the feather died. A similar process happens with the hair and nails of humans. Some of the 'never-lived' objects, such as the car, can move but they need to be driven by a person using fuel or to be allowed to roll down a slope. A car cannot reproduce and make a family of smaller cars!

Working with children Photographs or pictures can be used to carry out the same activity with children but it is much better to use the real objects. A collection of suitable items can be made from home which the children can handle as well as look at. Care should be taken with the choice of living things and these need to be in suitable containers. A few garden snails in a transparent plastic box would be interesting for the children to study. Let the children talk about each of the objects, sharing their thoughts and ideas before they sort the objects into the three sets.

Figure 5.2 Encouraging discussion about the objects to be sorted

Safety points

- Some children are allergic to furry animals.
- Certain plants can cause skin irritations.
- Wild mammals and birds, dead or alive, should not be used in school because they may carry disease.

Humans as organisms

The human body has to take in the energy and materials needed to stay alive and to get rid of the waste it produces. So that this can happen the millions of cells which make up the body are adapted to carry out particular jobs and grouped together to form organs such as the heart, kidneys, liver and brain. To enable these organs to work efficiently they are each part of a system. These systems have to work together to keep the body healthy. Things enter the body through the lungs and the digestive system and if we take in the wrong things we can become ill. Our bodies can also suffer if harmful substances or micro-organisms enter through the skin.

Table 5.1 The main body systems and their functions

Name of the organ system	Parts of the body	Purpose of the system
Digestive	Mouth, stomach, gut	Feeding and digesting food
Circulatory	Heart, blood vessels	Transporting materials around the body
Sensory and nervous	Skin, eyes, ears, tongue, nerves	Letting the body know what is happening outside so it can respond to changes
Respiratory	Mouth, nose, lungs, cells	Breathing and getting energy from food
Reproductive	Ovaries, uterus, vagina (female) testes, penis (male)	Producing eggs and sperm that can be used to make a baby
Endocrine	Various glands	Producing hormones which affect many different processes such as growth and development
Excretory	Kidneys, liver, skin	Getting rid of waste from cells
Musculo-skeletal	Muscles, bones	Supporting and protecting the body and enabling it to move

Activity 5.2 Healthy lifestyles Visit your local health centre, library and pharmacist and collect any free leaflets that are intended to encourage people to lead a healthier lifestyle. Use these to help you make a list of the ways in which we can take responsibility for keeping our bodies healthy.

Discussion There may be many different views on what makes up a healthy lifestyle and adults sometimes choose to ignore warnings from health authorities for a variety of reasons. So that children can make their own decisions when they are older they need to be given certain information about their bodies. In some cultures discussion about the parts of the body and its functions may be taboo. Anyone undertaking work with children concerning the human body needs to be aware of and follow the school policy on personal and social education (PSE) in conjunction with the rest of the staff.

Working with children Children will already be aware that they need food and drink to stay alive and they may know some of the parts of the human body. They may hold rather confused ideas about what constitutes a healthy diet for young children. As the quantity and types of food needed by the body vary depending on a person's age, size and lifestyle some young children might be drinking low fat milk when they should be having full milk. There are a number of activities that can be done with children to help them find out more about their bodies and how to keep them healthy.

- Discuss the external parts of the body and label a picture of a child dressed for school.
- Look at the contents of their lunch boxes and talk about the different foods.
- Look at pictures of the children as babies and discuss how they have changed.

- Let the children eat different flavoured crisps whilst holding their noses. Do the crisps taste different?
- Make a 'feely box' by decorating a cardboard box and provide a hole for the children to put their hands into it. Put a variety of items into the box and allow the children to discover if they can tell you what is in the box by just using their sense of touch. Encourage discussion of what they can feel so that other children in the group can try to guess what the object is.

Figure 5.3 Using the 'feely box'

The safety aspects of this work can be found in Chapter 3; please read them in conjunction with this section.

Green plants as organisms

Green plants, like all living things, need water and nutrients to grow. They also need oxygen. A pot plant will have different parts:
- the roots that grow into the soil to take up water and to support the stem;
- the stem which supports the leaves and flowers;
- the leaves which allow light and gases to pass through them;
- the flowers which produce seeds.

The plant will grow if it is given water and allowed to have light. Plants use light energy, carbon dioxide (a gas in the air) and water to make their own food in a process called photosynthesis. A houseplant may look weak and yellowish in colour if it does not get enough sunlight. It will also look healthier if it is given a 'plant food' because this contains chemicals which plants would normally get in the wild from natural compost. A carrot plant will store the extra food it has made in its root so that it can live through the winter. If the carrot was left in the ground it would grow and flower, producing seeds, during the following year.

Plants are very important to the animal kingdom because:
- much of the world's food comes directly from plants in the form of grains (wheat, oats, maize) which are processed to make flour;
- rice and potatoes form the staple diet of many people;
- animals that are farmed are also fed on plants;
- plants produce oxygen and use up carbon dioxide.

Activity 5.3 Growing seeds Try growing some seeds in a transparent container, with cotton wool instead of soil to give the children the opportunity to observe how plants develop. Cress seeds will start to swell as soon as they are wetted and will produce leaves in a few days if they are kept damp and warm. Runner bean seeds and broad bean seeds are much larger and it is easier to see the different parts developing. They will even produce flowers if kept for several weeks with sufficient light and water.

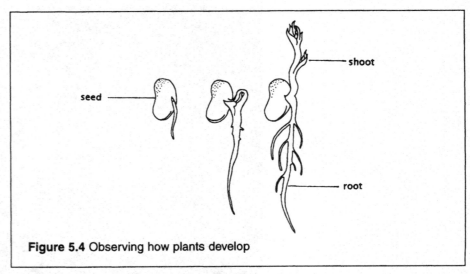

Figure 5.4 Observing how plants develop

Discussion The speed at which the plants will grow will depend on the amount of light and warmth they receive. You may like to try to grow more seeds but in the dark or in a cold place and see how these conditions affect their growth.

Safety points
- Packaged seeds are covered in fungicide to protect them from going mouldy.
- Hands must be washed after touching seeds.

Variation and classification

Scientists have developed several ways of grouping or classifying living things. A system proposed by a Swedish naturalist, Carolus Linnaeus, in 1735 divided the living world into two kingdoms, Plants and Animals. As more information was gathered about the different organisms, especially the ones that could only be seen clearly using a microscope, the classification system was revised to show three more kingdoms, Fungi, Protista and Bacteria.

Animals can be sorted into two groups, those with backbones (vertebrates) and those without backbones (invertebrates). The name 'minibeasts' is often used to describe very small animals found in the school grounds. This term does not refer to a particular group in a scientific sense but is a very useful word to use with children rather than 'insects' because not all the small creatures they may find belong to the group 'insects'. Snails are molluscs and spiders are arachnids (remember the film *Arachnaphobia*!).

Children are often more familiar with the vertebrate groups – fish, amphibians, reptiles, birds and mammals. They can use the features they see to decide which group an animal belongs to, although sometimes this can be difficult. A dolphin looks like a fish but is actually a mammal because it has lungs, is warm blooded and gives birth to live young which are suckled.

Activity 5.4 Grouping animals Use the classification chart to help you decide which groups the animals belong to on Activity sheet 6.

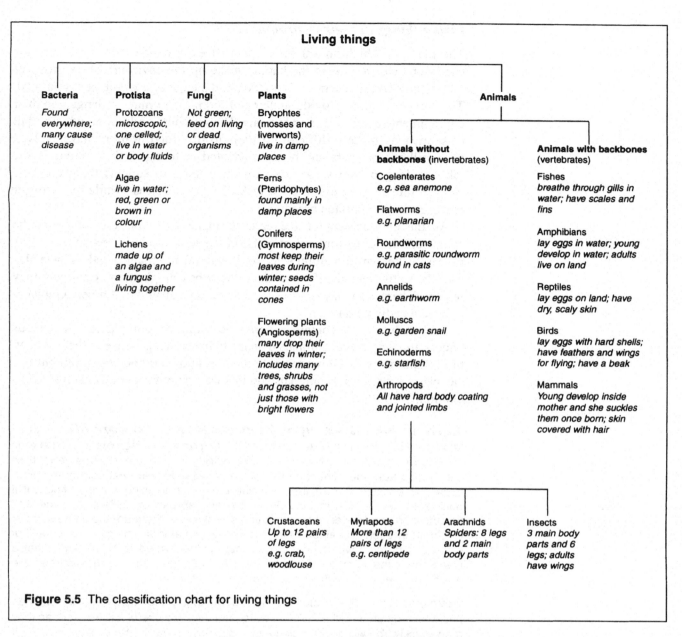

Figure 5.5 The classification chart for living things

Discussion Some of the names of the animals can be misleading. A starfish is not a fish but belongs to the invertebrate group echinoderms. You may feel that there are many animals that do not fit the most obvious group but there are only a few which need to remembered. Most birds fly but some, such as ostriches and penguins which have feathers and lay eggs, cannot fly.

Working with children Children are expected to group animals using observable features, so they will need to have pictures or photographs to sort. Ask them to suggest ways in which the animals could be grouped. These will not be the 'scientific' classifications but that does not matter because the activity is designed to encourage them to use their observational skills and discuss the similarities and differences of the animals in the pictures. When they are older they will be encouraged to use the classification system. Young children may suggest the following groupings for the animals:

- those which have four legs and those which have two;
- those which live in water and those which live on land;
- those which have fur, feathers or scales.

Living things in their environment

The place in which an animal or plant lives is called its habitat, and the conditions which exist in the habitat make up the environment. A group of rabbits may live in a series of burrows, at the edge of a wood, next to a field. They use the area to provide shelter and food. There may be dangers in their environment such as foxes or humans. The weather conditions, such as a fall of snow, may make it difficult for them to find food. Rabbits have evolved over millions of years and become adapted to living in this habitat. If the rabbit colony becomes too large for the habitat to support them then the weaker animals may die through lack of food or disease while the stronger ones survive to continue breeding.

As the environment of the earth changed over millions of years the characteristics of various animals also changed to produce new species. This process is known as 'natural selection'. Animal and plant breeders have also used 'selective breeding' to produce the types of plants and animals they require. There are many different breeds of dogs available if a person wishes to have a pedigree animal.

Each habitat will contain a variety of animals and plants. To help us understand why certain animals manage to live and reproduce in their habitat, the conditions in that environment could be studied in the classroom but this can cause distress to the animals and this would not be a good example to the children.

Activity 5.5 Does light help duckweed to spread? A plant known as duckweed can often be found floating on the surface of ponds. It seems to spread by making new plants very quickly during the summer and then disappears from the surface in the winter. It will reappear next spring and soon cover the surface of the water. You can carry out an experiment to find out if duckweed needs light to be able to live and spread by collecting some and floating it on pond water, in two containers. Make sure there are the same number of plants in each container. Keep these two containers next to each other but cover one of them with a shoebox so that the 'duckweed' is in the dark. After a week count the number of plants in each container. Which plants spread the most, the ones in the light or the ones in the dark?

Discussion These plants may not be thought of as plants by children because they are small and live in water, but they are useful for this work as they grow quickly. You will not be able to do this activity in the winter unless you collect some duckweed in the autumn and keep it in a container indoors.

Working with children Children will be looking at the animals and plants that live in different habitats in the local environment and how these environments might be different. Some habitats that can be studied include:

- school playing fields;
- hedgerows;
- trees and shrubs;
- a pile of small logs;
- a pond;
- a flowerbed.

Working outside with a small group of children looking for minibeasts can be very interesting but there are also a number of potential hazards that are explained in detail in Chapter 3. You should be sure that you know what these hazards are and how to deal with them before accompanying children outside.

Notes to leaders

- Discuss the outcomes of Activity sheet 5.
- Provide a suitable collection of living and non-living objects for the group to sort in the same way as with Activity sheet 5.
- Allow small groups the resources to find out more about one of the organ systems outlined in Table 5.1. They can share their findings with the rest of the group.
- Arrange for a suitable professional such as a health promotions officer or nutritionalist to visit the group and discuss ideas about healthy lifestyles.
- Provide a display of fruits and vegetables and ask the assistants to identify which part of a plant each came from.
- Encourage the assistants to build up a collection of pictures of plants and animals from magazines and seed catalogues to use with children.
- Discuss the different types of habitats for 'minibeasts' found in the grounds of the students' own workplaces. Devise ways of providing artificial habitats for those settings which have limited outside facilities.

Supporting understanding

Resources for working with children

Creary, C. and Wilson, G. (1996) *You, Me and Us.* Northampton: Northamptonshire Sciences Resources.
Morris, J. (1996) *Themes for Early Years – Growing.* Leamington Spa: Scholastic.
Patterson, J. (1996) *Schools' Organic Gardens.* Hatfield: The Association for Science Education.
Richards, R. (1989) *An Early Start to Nature.* Hemel Hempstead: Simon and Schuster.
Wade, W. and Hughes, C. (1991) *Inspirations for Science.* Leamington Spa: Scholastic.

Television programmes

BBC

Cat's Eyes: *Living; Night life; Being healthy; Movement; Survival; Plants and animals; Is it living?; Flowers, seeds and plants; Animal families; Animal care.*

Channel 4

Fourways Farm: *Three of a kind; Birth and death; Sickness and health.*
Stage One: the *Ourselves* unit – *Moving on, Skin deep, Seeing is believing, Hear this, Open wide*; the *Life and Living* unit – *Starting life, Growing, Life and death.*

Further reading

Farrow, S. (1996) *The Really Useful Science Book.* London: Falmer Press.
Kennedy, J. (1997) *Primary Science Knowledge and Understanding.* London: Routledge.
Nuffield Primary Science. (1997) *Understanding Science Ideas.* London: Collins.

Videos for background knowledge

Life and living processes, from the *Making Sense of Science* series (1995) Channel 4.
Life; diversity and evolution, from the *Teaching Today* series (1995) BBC.

Software

Plantwise (1994) Sherston Software. Malmsbury.
Bodywise (1995) Sherston Software. Malmsbury.

CHAPTER 6

Materials and their properties

Although the word 'material' is used in everyday language to mean 'fabric', it has a much wider scientific meaning. The term 'material' describes the substances from which things are made; a spoon, for example, may be made of wood, plastic or metal. To enable young children to make sense of this work the materials are often presented as part of familiar objects so the object may be a spoon but the material it is made of will be a metal such as stainless steel.

The key ideas covered in this chapter are:
- that there is a range of materials suitable for children to study;
- that each of these materials has certain properties that are special to that particular material;
- that some of these properties are also shown by other materials;
- that the properties of each material are related to how it can be used;
- that children need to gain first-hand experience of some of these materials so that they can discover some of the properties for themselves;
- that children will be able to use the first-hand information they have gained about each of the materials along with other ways of gaining information to make informed choices as to which materials are most suitable for a particular item or task;
- that some materials may be changed by heating or cooling;
- that the shape of some materials can be changed.

Children's early experiences

A baby will experience the feel of soft clothes against her skin, in contrast to the hardness of a teething ring as she takes it into her mouth. She will notice that there are toys of different colours, that many objects are shiny and some are furry. Young children use their sense of touch to discover the texture of objects and will shake or throw an object to discover if it makes a noise. They will investigate the 'squashability' of a new item by squeezing it. If it is a soft toy then it will usually go back to its original shape after this treatment. If the item being squashed is a biscuit, the shape will be destroyed and cannot be restored. It will still be edible but the small pieces may get spread over the floor instead of being eaten.

Adult carers will normally keep breakable items away from young children because of the dangers presented by the broken object. Children may break a toy or see an adult drop a piece of crockery. The idea of 'broken' is not an easy concept for a young child to understand. Sometimes the toy can be repaired but often this is not possible and this can be very upsetting for the child. Many items used by young children these days are made of plastics and so some children have limited experiences of natural items and their textures such as wood, stone, metals, fur and feathers.

Young children may have some experience of 'helping' to prepare food and cooking but they will have been concentrating on the end result and will not have thought about how the ingredients change when processed and cooked. Many families rely heavily on ready-prepared food and so some children may not have seen food such as cakes prepared from the original ingredients of eggs, flour, fat and milk.

Building key concepts

Grouping materials

Children can be introduced to the idea of sorting and grouping materials by using everyday objects. Part of this work links closely with sections of Chapter 5 in relation to the use of senses to explore and recognise differences and similarities between materials and put them into groups. In Chapter 5 the concepts of living and non-living were discussed and the focus was on the living world. In this chapter the ideas discussed will relate to things that 'never lived' and things that 'may once have been alive'. It is advisable to have carried out Activity 5.1 – 'Living or non-living' before reading this chapter.

What does the term 'properties' mean?

The term 'properties' is used to describe the characteristics that are special to that material, such as 'shiny' and 'smooth' for a metal spoon. These properties may also be shared by other materials.

Activity 6.1 What's in the bag? Collect together ten small household items and put them into a bag (or a 'feely box' as in Chapter 5). Choose objects that are safe to handle and which provide a variety of shapes and textures. Put your hand into the bag and pick up one of the objects, keeping it in the bag so that you cannot see it. Describe the texture of the object. What else can you tell about the object without looking at it? You will probably be able to name the object as you know which items were put into the bag. Take the object out of the bag. What else can you say about the object now that you can see it? Get a friend to choose ten different objects to put in the bag for you and repeat the activity. Is it more difficult to name the objects this time?

Discussion You probably felt a variety of textures, and words that you may have used include hard, soft, rough and smooth. There may have been a squashy object. If it returned to the original shape once you let go it has 'elasticity'. Some objects may be heavier than others of the same size and shape. A metal spoon will be heavier than a plastic spoon of the same size. When you took the article out of the bag you will have noticed its colour, size and shape. It may have been dull or shiny. Some materials, like clear plastic, allow the light through them (transparent). Others, like tissue paper, will let some light through (translucent).

Some of the objects may feel colder than the other items. Metals feel colder than plastics. All the items in the bag will have been at the same temperature (room temperature) but metals carry heat away from your hand better than plastics so the metal will feel colder. This demonstrates a property called thermal (or heat) conductivity and metals conduct heat well. Those items that do not conduct heat well are called thermal insulators. Air is a good thermal insulator and materials that can be formed to trap air become good insulators, such as 'bubble wrap' or 'thermal' underwear.

Working with children The last activity, 'What's in the bag', may be used with children to sort a variety of materials. Encourage children to look in the bag and ask:
- 'What colour is it?'
- 'It is shiny or dull?'
- 'Can you see through it?'

61

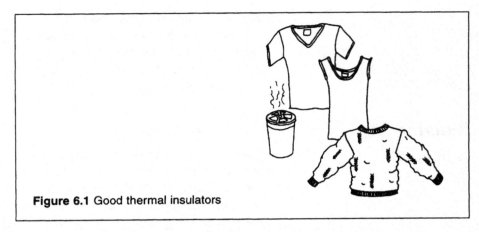

Figure 6.1 Good thermal insulators

Then the texture can be investigated by using the sense of touch:
- 'What does it feel like?'
- 'Is it hard or soft?'
- 'Is it smooth or rough?'
- 'Is it stiff or flexible?'

It might also be appropriate to use the following questions:
- 'Does it smell?'
- 'Does it bend?'
- 'Can you squash it?'
- 'Does it stick to a magnet?'

This work also gives opportunities to develop a child's vocabulary with the use of more open-ended questions as discussed in Chapter 4. Some of these questions can also be used to form the basis of an activity involving sets, for example, making a set of shiny items and a set of dull items.

Older children may be expected to use tests that result in breaking the material, 'testing to destruction', but these activities are not appropriate for younger children. To find out if something is bouncy (has elasticity) it would have to be dropped. If it were a football it would bounce. If the same was done with a lump of playdough it would probably be messy but not dangerous. If other items were used they might shatter or damage the floor. They could also cause injury to anyone standing nearby.

Figure 6.2 Sorting items into sets

Using collections

Everyday objects can be used to provide collections of items for children to observe, discuss and sort. It is important that they are allowed the 'real' items rather than pictures in the first instance and these need to be carefully selected so that they have the chosen properties. A collection of soft toys would not be very useful if the properties of hard or transparent were to be explored.

Activity 6.2 A collection of household objects Make a list of 20 household objects that would make a suitable collection for the children to sort if they were looking at texture, appearance and transparency. For each item, make a note of the important points that you would discuss with the children. Which groupings do you think children might use for your collection?

Working with children You should have made sure that each item would be safe for children to hold. The list should contain a good variety of items with different shapes, textures and colours. You should have included objects made from various materials such as wood, plastics, metals, wool, cotton and fabrics made of synthetic fibres. Children need to know about glass because it is such an important material in our lives. You could provide a small jam jar for the collection or talk about the glass in the classroom window instead. Coloured glass items can also add interest to a collection. (Read Chapter 3 for safety points.) Collections may be made of:

- different objects made from the same material, for example, a variety of wooden items such as a spoon, dish, animal figures, toy train, pencil;
- similar objects made from different materials, for example, spoons made of wood, metals and plastics.

Collections can also be made from a variety of objects that are familiar to the children such as:

- items found in the classroom;
- kitchen utensils;
- toys.

Changing materials

When children are exploring the properties of materials they may have tried to bend or squash them. In doing so they may have changed the shape of the object, but the material that the object was made of will not have changed. A drinks can made from aluminium will still be made of this material even if it is squashed. The changes in shape that can be made by squashing, bending, twisting and stretching materials may prevent that object being used for its original purpose such as the aluminium drinks can, but these types of changes can also be helpful. There are times when the shape of something is changed temporarily. If using a sponge to wash the car it is possible to use the sponge to follow the shape of the car's bodywork. Once the grime is removed the dirty sponge can be squeezed out in the bucket of water to clean it.

Many household items rely on the 'stretching' ability of coils and springs, such as those in armchairs and beds, as well as the tension created when a piece of metal is bent, for example in a shoe stretcher or clothes peg. Some clothes also contain materials that stretch and return to their original shape, such as those with elastic or containing Lycra.

Solids, liquids and gases

Materials can be changed by heating or cooling them. Heating can change their state from a solid to a liquid and from a liquid to a gas. Cooling can reverse these changes.

Figure 6.3 Common items which will stretch when put under strain and then return to their original shape

Water

Water, a liquid, will become ice, a solid, when put in a freezer. If this ice is then removed from the freezer and left on the kitchen table it will melt and become water again. If water is put into a pan on the cooker and heated it will change into water vapour, a gas, when it boils. If that water vapour meets a cold surface such as the glass in a window the water vapour will change back into liquid water and run down the glass. This is called 'condensation'. Water vapour is a colourless gas so it cannot be seen. The 'steam' seen coming from the spout of a kettle is formed as the water vapour meets the cold air and forms water droplets seen as a 'white cloud'.

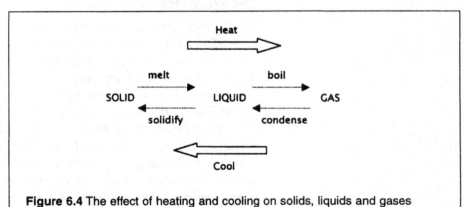

Figure 6.4 The effect of heating and cooling on solids, liquids and gases

Evaporation

Water can also become water vapour by a process called 'evaporation'. A damp towel left in the bathroom will eventually become dry because the liquid water in the towel will evaporate into the air. To dry the towel more quickly it could be hung on a warm radiator so that 'evaporation' happens more rapidly. Water is a very special substance because it is able to exist as a solid, a liquid and a gas in the temperatures found normally on earth.

Activity 6.3 Looking at solids, liquids and gases Make a collection of food and cleaning items from your kitchen cupboards as shown on Activity sheet 7. Sort them into examples of solids, liquids and gases. Are there any that you find difficult to put into a group?

Discussion A solid material is one that has a definite shape. Foods that keep their shape when placed on a plate, such as cheese and chocolate, would be examples of solids. If these solids are heated they will spread out and become liquid. Some of the solids are made into small grains, such as sugar and coffee granules. They will spread out if put on a plate but are still solids because each of the tiny grains has a definite shape. The liquids include vinegar and orange juice. Children often recognise 'washing- up liquid' as an example of a liquid because the word is part of its name. Tomato sauce is a thicker liquid.

Aerosols such as furniture polish contain propellant gases that push the liquid polish out as a fine spray of droplets of liquid when the button is pressed. More people are using pump action sprays, which use air, because of the environmental problems that some propellants can cause. The 'fizzy' drink contains the gas carbon dioxide, which starts to come out of the liquid as bubbles when the top of the bottle is removed.

Working with children This activity can be carried out with children. Check that the examples you select are safe for them to handle. Many cleaning materials would not be suitable for working with children because they would be harmful to them if spilt (see Chapter 3). Some children may be allergic to the perfumes in soaps and other toiletries. Ensure that the children do not spray aerosols into their eyes; the use of aerosols is best demonstrated by an adult.

The effect of heat on everyday materials

Heat has different effects on different substances. It can:
- change a solid to a liquid, for example melting butter;
- change a liquid to a gas, for example boiling water.

These changes can be reversed and so they are called temporary (or physical) changes. Heat may also affect materials in ways that cannot be reversed and these are known as permanent (or chemical) changes.

Making a cake is a good example of permanent change because the different ingredients are mixed and cooked. You cannot get the egg back out of either the raw cake mixture or the baked cake.

Activity 6.4 What's cooking? Activity sheet 8 gives a list of foods and the cooking methods. You have probably used all these methods in the past. Did you notice all the changes that took place in relation to the appearance and texture of the foods as they were cooked? Can you decide which of the examples are permanent changes?

Discussion When an egg is boiled it turns solid because its chemical structure is changed. Cooking vegetables in boiling water makes them softer to eat. Frying foods usually results in a change of colour. Fat in bacon becomes more transparent as it cooks. Cooking oil becomes more 'runny' (less viscous) as it gets hotter. If it starts to smoke it is dangerously hot and may start to burn causing a fire. The cooking oil can be cooled and re-used as it does not change permanently unless it gets too hot. Butter melts when heated a little but separates into different parts if heated for longer. Most of the changes that happen when food is cooked are permanent because the heating changes the chemical composition of the food.

When 'ice-pops' are frozen, the liquid inside the plastic sachets – mostly water – turns to ice. This process can be repeatedly reversed but it is not advisable to refreeze food once it has been thawed because of health hazards. Micro-organisms which may be in the food will grow and multiply as the food thaws. The food must be cooked to kill the bacteria. The cooked food can then be frozen.

Working with children Children enjoy using food and many activities are suitable for carrying out in school. Adult supervision is needed and hygienic conditions must be maintained. Details of these procedures are given in Chapter 3; please read them in conjunction with this section.

Natural and synthetic

The materials which children meet in their normal surroundings are both those which are in their original form, such as stone, and those which have been processed in some way, such as glass. Children will not have an understanding of whether a material occurs naturally or whether it has been purified or processed before use. Many materials found in the home or classroom have been manufactured by chemically changing the raw materials. Young children have difficulty in understanding the difference between chemically changing something such as oil to produce plastics and making a wooden ruler which has been formed from a wooden tree. Children do not appreciate that the ruler is still made of the same natural material, wood, but in a new shape.

Mixing and separating materials

Permanent (or chemical) changes

When two or more substances are mixed they may react chemically with each other to produce one or more new substances. Bread making is an example of this process. The flour, water, yeast and salt are mixed together to form a lump of dough. When this is cooked it becomes bread. This is a permanent change and the ingredients cannot be separated.

Temporary (or physical) changes

- **Mixing and sieving**. If gravel is mixed with sand they remain the same substances and if the correct size sieve is used the gravel can be separated from the sand. If the mixture is made up of a liquid and small pieces of solids such as tea leaves and water, then this method will still work using sieves and filters which have much smaller holes in them.

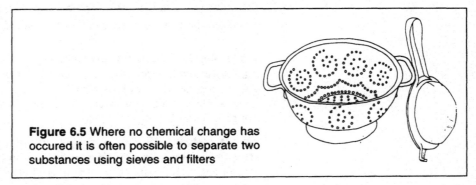

Figure 6.5 Where no chemical change has occured it is often possible to separate two substances using sieves and filters

- **Dissolving and evaporating**. If one substance dissolves in another, for example, sugar in water, a solution is formed. The sugar seems to 'disappear' but the sugar particles are still there. When sugar is added to a cup of tea and stirred, the crystals dissolve and make the tea taste sweet. The sugar can be retrieved from the solution by letting the water evaporate into the air. If a shallow dish of sugar solution is left in a warm place, such as a sunny window sill, then small crystals of sugar will be left when the water evaporates.

Activity 6.5 Does it dissolve? Activity sheet 9 outlines how you can investigate whether some common substances from home dissolve in water.

Discussion You probably found that the salt dissolves most easily in the water. The sugar and coffee granules also dissolve with stirring. The tea leaves will not dissolve completely but you will have noticed that some colour came from the leaves, so something did dissolve. Some parts of the flour dissolve in the water but flour is also left at the bottom of the container. The cooking oil floats on the top of the water and even if you mix it with the water it will still separate.

You may wish to repeat the investigation with the same substances and warm water. You will find that using warm water makes everything happen more quickly and may result in more of the substance dissolving except for the cooking oil. In this work the substance that dissolves, for example salt, is called the solute and the substance that it dissolves in, water, is called the solvent. There are other solvents apart from water, but they are not used in primary schools because they are too dangerous to health.

Working with children Young children usually say that the sugar 'disappears' if it is added to water. The ideas met in this work are more appropriate for older children but young children may experience some aspects of this work through simple activities such as making milkshakes. By using foods in a hygienic setting, they can appreciate the change in taste.

Cleaning clothes

Oil or grease does not dissolve in water so other solvents such as perchlorethylene are used to remove grease from clothes. Some clothes manufactures recommend that items should not be washed because the fabric may be damaged. They recommend 'dry cleaning' where the solvent used is not water.

Detergents and soaps are used to remove grease from clothes and plates because they act chemically on the grease to allow the water to act temporarily as a solvent. The grease is carried away by the water if the sink is emptied whilst the water is still hot and bubbly. If the water is left to get cold, the bubbles disappear and the grease floats to the top of the water.

Activity 6.6 Making playdough You can use the following recipe to make a type of playdough which will last for several months if kept in an airtight container while not in use. While you are making it think about what is happening to the ingredients in relation to what you have learned about 'materials' from this chapter.

Cooked playdough ingredients
One cup of flour
Half a cup of cooking salt
One cup of water
One tablespoon of cooking oil
One teaspoon of cream of tartar
A few drops of food colouring

Put all the ingredients into a saucepan and cook the mixture over a medium heat. Stir the mixture with a wooden spoon all the time so that it does not burn. The mixture will be a liquid for a while and just as you start to wonder if you have made a mistake it will suddenly start to turn solid. When the mixture comes away from the side of the pan, remove it from the heat. Allow the lump of dough to cool a little, so that you do not burn yourself, and then knead the dough thoroughly. If your dough is still sticky then it may need heating for longer. Put the pan to soak to make it easier to clean.

Discussion The ingredients you used were solids and liquids which, when mixed, formed a thick liquid in the pan. The effect of heating that mixture was to make it solidify into a lump of dough. You probably added some air, a gas, to the mixture when you stirred the mixture and then kneaded the dough. The changes made to the ingredients were permanent.

Working with children This cooked dough can be used to demonstrate permanent changes to children without needing to address the hygiene issues concerned with food. The heating of the dough needs to be carried out by the adult with the children observing. They may help stir the mixture if this can be done without risk of injury. Once the dough has cooled sufficiently, the children can carry out the kneading. Larger quantities of the dough can be made in different colours. There are recipes available to make various types of dough which show different properties; many of these describe uncooked dough, which does not last as long as the cooked varieties, but does not require the use of a hotplate. Working with dough presents many opportunities for development of language skills and mathematical skills as well as exploration of materials.

Notes to leaders

- Discuss the outcomes of Activity 6.1 and devise a list of the most interesting objects to use.
- Encourage assistants to make and decorate their own 'feely box' or 'feely bag' and use it with children.
- Ask assistants to work in pairs to make a collection of items based on a specific theme such as 'paper' or 'brushes' and explain how this collection can be used for science work on materials.
- Suggest that each assistant brings a toy to the session and use this collection as a starting point for work on materials.
- Ask each assistant to bring a copy of a recipe that they have found to be successful when preparing food with children. Suggest that they use a variety of cooked and uncooked foods with children.
- Collect a variety of playdough recipes. The assistants can make these up and compare the properties of the different types.

Supporting understanding

Resources for working with children

NIAS (1996) *Chemistry and Cookery*. Northampton: Northamptonshire Inspection and Advisory Service.

NIAS (1996) *All Sorts of Stuff*. Northampton: Northamptonshire Inspection and Advisory Service.

Richards, R. Collis, M. and Kincaid, D. (1990) *An Early Start to Science*. Hemel Hempstead: Simon and Schuster.

Television programmes

BBC

Cat's Eyes: *Changing materials*; *Freezing and melting*; *The effects of heat*; *Bending*; *Giving things shape*.

Channel 4

Stage One: *Materials We Need* series: *Paper*; *Fabric*; *Clay*; *Plastic*.

Further reading

Farrow, S. (1996) *The Really Useful Science Book*. London: Falmer Press.

Kennedy, J. (1997) *Primary Science Knowledge and Understanding*. London: Routledge.

Nuffield Primary Science (1997) *Understanding Science Ideas*. London: Collins Educational.

Video for background knowledge

Materials and *Changing Materials* from the *Making Sense of Science* series (1995) Channel 4.

CHAPTER 7

Physical processes

This chapter considers the following key ideas:
- that children should be taught about the importance of electricity at home and in school and should have an understanding of the dangers concerned with its misuse.
- that children should have opportunities to construct simple electric circuits with batteries, wires, bulbs and buzzers and to appreciate that these will not work if there is a break in the circuit.
- that children begin to appreciate that forces can make things speed up, slow down or change direction and that pushes and pulls are examples of forces.
- that children can appreciate that forces can change the shape of objects.
- that children understand that darkness is the absence of light and that light comes from a variety of sources.
- that children have experience of many kinds and sources of sound.
- that children appreciate that sounds are heard when they enter the ear and that sounds travel away from sources, getting fainter as they do so.

Children's early experiences

Children have lived in the physical world since before they were born. An unborn child in the mother's womb is provided with a warm, safe environment in which to develop. She is still affected by the force of gravity and can hear sounds. The birth usually involves sustained pushing by the mother as the child is forced into the world. Soon after the birth the child's senses are stimulated by the light and sounds of the environment.

In the first few years of children's lives they spend much of their time exploring the physical environment and experiencing in an informal way the phenomena which they will study in a more systematic way later on. A baby's attention is gained more quickly by a moving object than one that is still. If an object is shiny and reflects light it will be more attractive to a young child than a dull object. Children's attention can also be gained by the use of sounds. The most basic hearing tests involve attracting a child's interest in an object or person in front of them while another adult makes a sound behind or to one side of the child. A child with normal hearing will turn to look at the source of the sound. Toy manufacturers incorporate the production of light, sound and movement into many toys. Children will be interested in these types of toys when they first see them but unless the child can interact with the toy they may lose interest. This type of toy often requires batteries so children also come to understand that the toy will not work without a source of power. Children gain first-hand experiences of forces in action as they pull and stretch their clothes when getting dressed. They will also have some experience of how objects behave in water by playing with objects in a water tray and in the bath.

Figure 7.1 Children experience the forces associated with floating and sinking when working at the water tray

Building key concepts

Electricity

Many appliances and pieces of equipment at home and work rely on electricity as a source of power. This power source may be from mains electricity or batteries.

Activity 7.1 Electrical appliances Think about the electrical items that you use as you go through a normal day at home or at school. Make a list of the appliances you use in your home and in school that rely on mains electricity as a power source. You could make a separate list of those that use battery power instead of mains power. Some will have both. You could then tick those that you would consider essential for a modern household.

Discussion You will see from your list that there is heavy reliance on electricity at home. Most homes use electricity for lighting, entertainment, and some for cooking and heating. Even if gas is used for heating and cooking, some appliances still use electricity to enable them to work correctly. In a power cut people cannot use their gas central heating boilers because electricity is needed for them to work. Some appliances such as torches are provided with separate batteries as a power source. Other items, such as mobile phones, have an internal battery which is charged from the mains using a transformer so that the appliance can work for a certain length of time without being connected directly to the mains. Whether you regard certain items as essential to your lifestyle will depend on your experiences and your personal viewpoint. As modern life becomes busier and traditional roles within the family change, priorities change. As scientists and technologists develop new labour-saving products so the list of electrical household items gets longer.

Working with children This work can be carried out with children using pictures from catalogues of household items and toys. Children can choose the pictures of electrical items but they will probably need help from an adult in reading and interpreting the description of the item. A pair of kitchen scales can be mechanical or electronic and children will need to discuss the difference because the electronic scales will need a battery. The children might sort the items in relation to the room in their house in which the items are normally used. In doing this they will notice that none of the portable electrical items should appear in the bathroom. This observation can lead to work on safety in relation to electricity.

Activities involving electricity can be great fun but they need to be set in a safe context (see Chapter 3). Teachers begin this topic with a discussion on safety with regards to mains electricity in the home and school. There are a number of video programmes that are particularly useful in illustrating the potential dangers to young children in a way that they can understand and appreciate. After viewing a programme children can be asked to make a poster warning others about the potential dangers of mains electricity.

Safety and electricity

The safety issues in relation to the use of electricity in schools are discussed in Chapter 3; please read these before proceeding with this work.

Making circuits

At Key Stage 1 children are expected to be able to make simple circuits with batteries, wires, bulbs and buzzers. In making them on different occasions and in different contexts they will come to appreciate that their circuits will not work if they are not complete. It is not always easy to see if component parts of a circuit are broken and so children should test each part before putting them together. If they do this before trying to make up the circuit then it will become easier to check for poor connections between the components.

Activity 7.2 Making circuits You will need the electrical components shown in Figure 7.2. Use a 4.5V (volt) battery, two wires and a 3V or 6V bulb to make a circuit and make the bulb light. Notice that the battery has two distinct metal parts, one labelled + (positive) and one labelled − (negative). These parts are called terminals. Try reversing the terminal connections to the bulb. Does it make any difference? Replace the bulb with the buzzer. Does it work? Try reversing the connections again. Does the buzzer work this time?

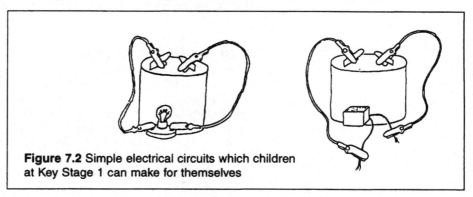

Figure 7.2 Simple electrical circuits which children at Key Stage 1 can make for themselves

Discussion This type of battery is simple to use with young children because they can make the connections easily. Crocodile clips on the wires help to make a firmer connection and using a bulb holder for the bulb prevents it being damaged. The bulb should light when the battery is reversed but some buzzers will only work one way round. You have made a simple circuit with either a bulb or a buzzer. The electrical components work because the electric current flows from one terminal of the battery, through the metal wire to the bulb, through the bulb and along the other metal wire to the other terminal. Tiny particles called electrons, which are present in the wire all the time, start moving more quickly and in a particular direction when the wire is part of a circuit which contains a battery. This flow of electrons is called an electric current. The size of the electric current is measured in amperes (A) and is the same all around the circuit.

The battery provides the energy, measured in volts (V) to 'push' the electrons around the circuit. Inside the battery there are chemicals which react together to provide the electrical energy. When these chemicals are used up, the reaction stops, the voltage of the battery drops and it cannot provide the energy required to light the bulb.

Figure 7.3 Encourage children to check each part of the circuit as they put it together

Activity 7.3 Conductors and insulators As you have already discovered, metal wires will conduct electricity and are examples of good electrical conductors. The opposite of a conductor is an insulator (heat insulators are discussed in Chapter 6). Some materials are electrical conductors and others are electrical insulators. Use Activity sheet 10: make a circuit and use it to test the materials given to find out which allow electricity to pass through them.

Discussion All metals, such as steel, copper and aluminium, are conductors of electricity. The pencil 'lead' is made of a form of carbon called graphite which also conducts electricity. These substances are good conductors because they contain a large number of electrons that are free to move when they are part of an electric circuit. Materials such as plastics, rubber and glass have no free electrons and are electrical insulators. At the low voltage used in school, air is a very poor conductor. If there is an air gap in the circuit, a break in the circuit or a loose connection then the electricity will not be able to flow and the bulb will not light. A switch makes an air gap in a circuit so that the electricity can be controlled.

Activity 7.4 Looking at light bulbs more closely Carefully unscrew the bulb from the bulb holder and take a closer look at it. Use a hand lens to look for the filament shown in Figure 7.4. Compare it with a normal sized, clear light bulb. A current flows more easily through a thick piece of wire than it does through a thin piece of the same type. When the bulb is put into a circuit the filament, which is a very thin piece of wire, has a high resistance and gets so hot that it glows and produces light. It does not burn away because there is no oxygen inside the glass bulb to allow it to burn. If the voltage of the battery is much greater than the voltage of the bulb then the filament gets too hot, melts and the bulb 'blows'. This breaks the circuit.

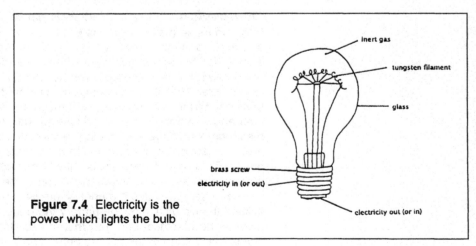

Figure 7.4 Electricity is the power which lights the bulb

Forces and motion

The word 'force' can be used in everyday language to describe things happening to people against their will, sometimes combined with violence. It can also imply that a lot of effort is needed to do something, such as 'My Mum forced me to tidy my room' and 'I had to force the shed door to close'. In science, 'force' means a push or a pull but it is often impossible to see this happening so people do not always appreciate that forces exist. Everything on earth is being acted upon by forces and in many cases these forces are 'balanced' so that there appears to be nothing happening. All objects on earth are affected by gravity, which is the pull of the earth on that object. A small child can sit on a nursery sized chair quite safely because the downward pull of the gravity on the child is balanced by an upward push on the child by the chair. If a very large adult tries to sit on a nursery chair the chair might break because the forces are unbalanced. The heavy adult cannot be supported by the small chair.

The downward pull of gravity is a force. This force is called weight and in science it is measured in units called newtons.

Figure 7.5 Goldilocks broke Baby Bear's chair when she sat upon it

Mass and weight

Young children will use the terms 'heavy' and 'light' and experience 'weighing' in grams and kilograms. They are trying to find the mass of an object or how much 'stuff' there is in the object. Mass is not usually measured directly. Instead, the pull of gravity on an object is measured in newtons. Weighing scales convert this into the mass of the object in kilograms. On Earth the pull of gravity on each kilogram is 10 newtons, so a bag of sugar with a mass of 1 kilogram has a weight of 10 newtons. An apple has a mass of about 100 grams and weighs about 1 newton.

The mass of an object remains the same whether it is on the Earth, on the Moon, or in space. The weight does change as the object moves away from the pull of the Earth's gravity. When the astronauts were on the Moon their mass was the same as on Earth but their weight changed because the pull of gravity on the Moon is much smaller than on Earth. Their weight was six times less on the Moon that it was on Earth, so if you want to lose weight then go to the Moon! Unfortunately, however, your mass will stay the same so you will still need the same size of clothes.

When an object floats in water the pull of gravity on the object pulling downwards is balanced by the upward force of the water called upthrust.

Upthrust is the force that makes things buoyant in water. Whether something floats depends on a combination of factors, which include:
- the material it is made of;
- its shape;
- the liquid it is in.

Although younger children will have opportunities to play with water and may experience 'floating and sinking' activities, they will not be expected to discuss the concept of 'upthrust' until Key Stage 2. The work with young children focusses on examples of unbalanced forces that result in something observable happening such as a toy moving or playdough changing shape.

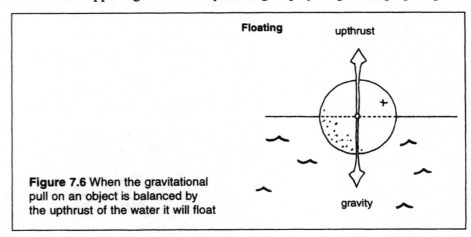

Figure 7.6 When the gravitational pull on an object is balanced by the upthrust of the water it will float

Activity 7.5 Toy cars moving Take a small toy car with wheels that move freely and give it a push on a tiled or wooden floor so that it travels a little way across the floor. Why did it stop? How can you make it go further? Push it again. Can you stop it before it comes to rest naturally? Can you make the car change direction once it is moving? What happens when you try to push the same car on a carpeted floor? Think about the forces that make the car move and those that make it slow down.

Discussion You supplied the force to start the car moving by pushing it. The car slowed down and stopped after you stopped pushing because of friction, a force that opposes the movement of one surface against another. Air resistance is a form of friction which the car met as it moved along, and there was also friction between the tyres and the floor. By pushing it harder you made it travel further across the floor and you could stop it by putting your hand or another object in its way. Making it change direction once it is moving is difficult if the wheels are fixed because if you touch the car it tends to stop. Often toy cars do not keep in straight lines because their wheels have been damaged by frequent use. On carpet the car experienced more friction between the carpet and the tyres so it did not move as quickly or as far as on the smooth floor.

Working with children This activity can be carried out with children and the discussion will provide opportunities to use the language required in this area.
- The car was pushed to start it moving.
- The car slowed down and stopped.
- The car will keep moving if we keep pushing it.
- The car moves more easily over a smooth floor than a carpet.
- The car can be stopped by putting something in its path.
- If a car is placed at the top of a ramp or slope, the pull of gravity is the force that starts the car moving.

Figure 7.7 Gravitational pull moves the car down the ramp

Starting things moving and stopping them

More force is needed to move an object with more mass than to move one of the same size that has less mass. A heavy football will stay put if children leave it on the grass on a windy day, but a beach ball, which is much lighter, might be blown away. It takes more force to slow down or stop an object with more mass so if a child is learning to catch a ball that has been rolled along the floor, a lighter ball such as a foam one is used rather than a cricket ball because the heavier ball might hurt her.

Changing shape

In Chapter 6 the ways in which materials can change shape was discussed and it is helpful to include discussion of the pushes and pulls or forces which are used to make these changes. In making bread or playdough children experience the force required to knead dough.

Activity 7.6 Forces in the home Look at the examples of everyday activities on Activity sheet 11. Think about the pulls and pushes that occur during these activities and complete the sheet.

Figure 7.8 The forces of push and pull are used to change the shape of the playdough

75

Discussion Each movement requires a push or a pull. Sometimes both are needed, as in the example of writing.

Working with children Children are familiar with getting dressed and they will be able to talk about 'pushing' their arm into a coat sleeve and 'pulling' their socks on. They may need to try sweeping with a broom if they have not had the chance at home. They will come to appreciate that it is sometimes pushed to collect the leaves and sometimes pulled to make a pile of leaves. Many children will still find writing a novel experience and will talk about the way in which they have to push and pull the pencil to form letters. Opening and closing doors and drawers are also examples of pushes and pulls with which children will be familiar. They will have many toys that need pushes or pulls to make them work.

Magnetic forces

In Chapter 6, materials were tested to find out if they were magnetic. Items containing iron, usually in the form of steel, will be magnetic. Other magnetic materials include cobalt and nickel, but these would not be found in school.

Activity 7.7 'Feeling' magnetic forces You will need a pair of bar magnets and, if possible, other types and shapes of magnets. The bar magnets may have different coloured ends or poles. What happens when you move the similar ends together? What happens when you put the opposite ends together? Does the same happen if you bring the end of one magnet to the middle of the other magnet? Try similar actions with the other magnets in your collection.

Figure 7.9 Magnets are stored with 'keepers' which help to retain the magnetism

Discussion When you put the similar ends, or poles, of the bar magnets together you should feel a force of 'repulsion'. The poles try to push away from each other. When the two opposite ends or poles are together they are attracted to each other and stick together. The force of repulsion is stronger at the ends of the bar magnet than in the middle. The other magnets may not show different coloured poles but you should still be able to find areas of attraction and repulsion between different ones. Ring magnets have their poles on their flat faces.

Working with children This activity can be carried out with children. Magnetic forces are examples of forces that children can feel and observe. The bar magnets need to be of good quality so that children can try to push the similar poles together. They should be encouraged to handle magnets carefully, as dropping or banging them will destroy their magnetism. Children may have a train set at home that uses magnetic force to join the carriages together. They may also have seen fridge magnets used to hold messages in place.

Light and sound

Light and dark

Many children in this country never experience complete darkness. Even at night there will be streetlights in towns and cities so that even when the lights are off inside the house, light still enters the room from outside. Children and adults will refer to this as 'darkness' but as their eyes and brain become accustomed to the low light intensity they are able to pick out various dark shapes. In total darkness they would see nothing because light must fall on an object for it to be seen. At Key Stage 1 children should experience a variety of light sources and this work links with topics such as electricity, heat and senses. Tell children that they must never look directly at the sun, even with sunglasses on, as this will cause permanent damage to their eyes.

Activity 7.8 Thinking about light sources Activity sheet 12 gives examples of objects that children suggested were sources of light. Which ones are sources that actually give out light? Which examples are reflecting light from another source?

Discussion The torch, lamp, television and spotlight are sources of light which use electricity. The candle, the sun and stars also produce light, as do some animals such as glow-worms, who produce light to attract a mate. The moon does not produce its own light. The glow of the moon is a result of light from the sun falling onto the moon and being reflected back to earth. The glow from cats-eyes in the road is reflected light from car headlights.

Working with children It is helpful if children observe a collection of objects that are light sources which they see working. These sources often produce heat as well as light so this work should be done under strict adult supervision to ensure safety. The safest light sources for children to handle are torches as these are made to be portable. To appreciate the full effect of these light sources work in a part of the classroom that does not have good natural light as it is difficult to see a candle flame when sunlight falls directly on to it. A darkened area can be constructed using large sheets of cardboard or dark curtains if the classroom does not have a walk-in cupboard.

Making and detecting sounds

Sounds can be heard for much of the time in daily life, and most children will have experienced a variety of them – both pleasant sounds and sounds that they do not like. People tend to ignore many of the background noises and concentrate on those that are most important to them. If a child shouts 'Mummy' in a supermarket many women will turn to look for the child, even those who do not have their own children with them at the time.

Activity 7.9 Listening carefully Sit with your eyes closed for a few minutes in a quiet place and listen to the sounds you can hear at school or at home. Open your eyes and make a list of the sounds.

Discussion You may not be able to work out the source of each sound but you can guess because you have had experience of similar sounds before. Even in a classroom that does not contain children you may be able to hear the heating system, the computer humming, children's voices in the playground, traffic noises and birds singing outside. These sounds have travelled to you through the air and through the materials that make up the building. Your ears have detected the tiny changes in the air and your brain has interpreted them as sounds.

Working with children The work on sound links closely with music, listening skills in English and with other science work on the senses and ourselves. Take children for a 'listening walk' and encourage them to draw a map giving their interpretation of the sounds that they hear. Encourage them to discuss 'useful' sounds which help them to find out more about the environment and those sounds which are not helpful to them. The safety aspects of loud noises can also be discussed here. An audio tape of everyday sounds can provide a good stimulus for work on sound.

Activity 7.10 Sounds travelling Put a portable radio (or a ringing alarm clock) in the middle of an open space such as the playground and then slowly walk away from it.

Discussion You will notice that the sound travels to your ear but it gets fainter as you move away from the source, the radio or clock. If you want to hear the radio more clearly then you have to move closer to it again. This will also happen in a building such as the school, but here, if you move to a different room, the materials of the building will also affect the way in which the sound travels. Soft materials such as curtains and carpets will absorb sounds. Hard surfaces such as walls will allow sounds to be reflected as echoes.

Working with children This activity can be used with children. Ask them to make a signal, such as putting their hands in the air, to show that they can hear the sound. When they have moved to a position in the playground where they can no longer hear the sound they put their hands down. Adults need to be sensitive to the fact that young children may suffer some temporary hearing loss when they have a cold, so there could be a variation in their ability to hear at different times in their early childhood.

Notes to leaders

- Arrange for the assistants to view one of the video programmes on the dangers of electricity and discuss its use with children.
- Look at a variety of torches by asking each assistant to bring a torch from home and take it apart to find out how it works.
- Discuss the use of magnets in the home. How many examples can the assistants find in their own homes?
- Discuss the items that would be suitable to form a collection for 'floating and sinking' at the water tray.
- Ask the assistants to show pictures of light sources to a small group of children and record their discussion. Encourage them to compare their observations with each other.
- Encourage the assistants to devise a child's game about 'sounds' and demonstrate it to the group.

Supporting understanding

Resources for working with children

Hughes, C. and Wade, W. (1991) *Bright Ideas – Inspirations for Science*. Leamington Spa: Scholastic.

NIAS (1998) *Push, Pull and Twist*. Northampton: Northamptonshire Inspection and Advisory Service.

Peacock, G. and Smith, R. (1992) *Teaching and Understanding Science*. London: Hodder and Stoughton.

Richards, R., Collis, M. and Kincaid, D. (1987) *An Early Start to Science*. Hemel Hempstead: Simon and Schuster.

Television programmes

BBC

Cat's Eyes: Forces – *Push and Pull*; Falling – *Floating and sinking, Natural forces*; Electricity – *Electricity helps, Electric shocks, Electricity past and present, Magnets*; Light and sound – *Light and dark, Colour, Sound, Music*.

Further reading

Kennedy, J. (1997) *Primary Science Knowledge and Understanding*. London: Routledge.

Nuffield Primary Science (1997) *Understanding Science Ideas*. London: Collins.

Videos for background knowledge

Electricity, Forces, Light, Sound from the *Making Sense of Science* series (1995) Channel 4.

CHAPTER 8

Technology processes

This chapter considers how children can be helped to develop their technological skills. They are encouraged to develop:
- skills in designing, including exploring materials and how they might use them, and making sketches and plans of their own design;
- skills in making, becoming more proficient in cutting, joining, folding, building and in using simple mechanisms, and in using materials and tools appropriately;
- knowledge and understanding of mechanisms, structures, products and applications; investigating products and learning how they function, understanding what is meant by quality, understanding of health and safety as consumers and technologists, and building a vocabulary to help them to describe and name equipment and materials and to discuss their work.

Children's early experiences

From a very early age, children begin to learn about objects and how they work. They put toys into their mouths and discover their taste, smell and texture, learn that some toys make a noise if they are shaken and, as they grow, begin to make their own structures using building bricks, early construction kits and everyday objects and materials. By the time they start pre-fives education they may well already be familiar with using paint, cutting, sticking, making models with plasticine, and digging and modelling in sand. These are excellent starting points for helping children to develop their technological skills.

Adults use their understanding of technology in everyday situations such as planning and preparing meals, planning and carrying out DIY projects at home, and enjoying hobbies including model-making, sewing and knitting – all of these involve adults in using technological skills and processes. In today's society we all, children and adults, use modern technological advances. Today's society is a technological one; the study of design and technology in school helps children to understand and use technological skills and processes.

Activity 8.1 Technology in everyday life Look around you at home and at work. What aspects of technology do you use in everyday living? What range of technological skills do you use? Make some lists.

Discussion Compare your lists with a friend or colleague. You will make use of many technological developments in everyday life, such as machinery including various forms of transport, electrical equipment in the home and communications technology. You will have many technological skills including cutting, measuring and sticking. You may be a keen gardener and design and make changes to your garden, or an eager cook who tries out new recipes or develops your own.

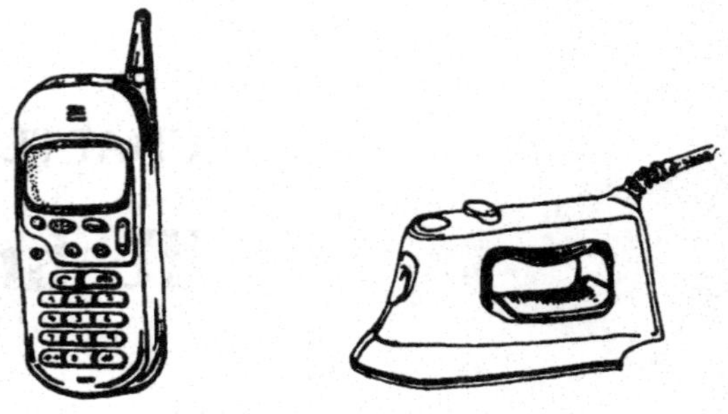

Figure 8.1 Products are based upon modern technological advances which have changed our lives dramatically

Working with children As you work through this chapter, identify skills and processes that you already use and those which are less familiar to you. Practise those that are less familiar so that you become more adept and can support the children as they work.

Building key skills

Using materials and tools

Children will be expected to learn how to use a wide range of tools and materials and how to choose the most appropriate material for the task. Encourage them to think about which materials would be suitable for a particular project and why. Ask them to describe the properties of the materials, using language such as bendy, stiff, strong. For some projects properties of water resistance will be important so encourage the children to predict which materials are waterproof and explain why they think so. This will help them to draw upon their everyday experiences, to make predictions, and then to devise a test to check their prediction.

Construction materials

These include sheet materials, items that can be assembled, items that form a framework and malleable materials. They are used to give children experience with working with a wide variety of materials so that they learn about why particular materials are chosen for specific use. The following are examples, not a complete list. Check in the store cupboard to see exactly what is used at school.

- Sheet materials: including paper, card, and corrugated plastic or paper.
- Items that can be assembled: some items will be reclaimed materials such as cardboard tubes, commercial packaging including boxes, cartons and plastic bottles, cotton reels, foil dishes and corks. Other items may be purchased, such as ready-cut wheels and gears.
- Items to make frameworks: straws, sticks, wooden dowelling and wire.
- Malleable materials: plasticine, playdough, clay and papier-mâché.

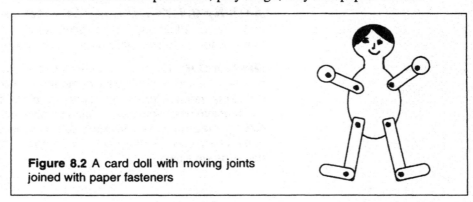

Figure 8.2 A card doll with moving joints joined with paper fasteners

Some reclaimed materials are banned by many LEAs, including egg boxes (risk of children catching egg-born disease, including salmonella), small pieces of polystyrene (risk of swallowing and choking or of young children poking them into their ears and noses), and inner cardboard tubes from toilet tubes (risk of children catching diseases including hepatitis). Check what may be used and what has been banned at school.

Construction kits and mechanical components

There are various commercially produced construction kits which help children to:

- make structures, such as walls, arches, bridges, and towers;
- make structures with moving parts, using gears and pulleys;
- design and make their own structures;
- follow instructions, spoken, written or from diagrams, to make models and to improve their assembly skills.

Figure 8.3 Children use commercially produced construction kits to make working models

With some kits children will experience using gears, pulleys, wheels and small electric motors, so that they make moving models such as cars, cranes or a clock face with moving hands.

Electrical components

Children may make simple electrical circuits to light a bulb or sound a buzzer, using electrical wire, batteries, bulbs, bulb holders and buzzers. This work links closely with work in science (see Chapter 7).

Textiles

Children learn to use textiles and study how these are used in the world around them. There are links with science, as children explore the properties of materials, such as finding a suitable fabric to make teddy a waterproof coat (see Chapter 6). They will use materials such as:

- fabrics;
- threads;
- trimmings.

They will experiment with printing and weaving (links to art), and learn how to cut and join fabrics for themselves, using their developing skills in measurement (links to mathematics).

Food

Food technology includes learning about food products and using ingredients in designing and making. Children learn about safety and hygiene when working with food. Check the requirements for safety and hygiene in the policy for working with food at school.

Gardening

Children may be involved in designing and making a garden, where they will use garden tools and handle plants and seeds. They will learn about suitable growing conditions for plants, and about making a garden attractive. This work links closely with science (see Chapter 5).

Using tools

Children will use a range of tools. The following list, with suggestions for safe and effective use, shows some of the tools that children will meet, but it is not exclusive. There is further guidance on health and safety and using tools to be found in Chapter 3.

- Scissors: rounded-end scissors for this age group; in Key Stage 2 pointed ended scissors may be used for specific tasks, such as cutting inside a sheet of paper or card. Left-handed children work more effectively with left-handed scissors. If you are right-handed, try cutting with a right-handed pair of scissors in your left hand – you will discover how difficult and uncomfortable this is and that it is not possible to see the cutting line with any degree of accuracy. This is how it feels for a left-handed child who uses a pair of right-handed scissors! There may be dual purpose scissors available which are suitable for either left- or right-handed children. Younger children begin by learning to use scissors safely, and will need to be taught how to carry them without harming themselves or others, holding them by the closed blades. Younger children may not have developed sufficient fine motor control to cut out with sufficient accuracy; they should be encouraged to follow cutting lines, if these are present. Through practice they will become more adept at cutting.
- Rulers, measuring tapes and weighing equipment: children who are just learning to measure benefit from using a ruler without a 'deadend' so that they can match the start of the measure with the end of the ruler. Choose weighing and measuring instruments with care so that children use those suitable for their ability with non-standard or metric units.

Figure 8.4 Instruments for weighing and measuring lengths

- Woodworking tools including hammer, hand-held drill and junior hacksaw, vice, woodworking bench, screwdriver, sandpaper, screws and nails: where children use a hammer or screw-driver, ensure that they work safely, and that the surface on which they work is protected by a thick piece of board. When using drills and saws, the work should be fixed in a vice or a woodworking bench to avoid accidents caused by the tools or the work slipping.
- Hole makers including bradawl and hole punch: where children need to make a hole, perhaps in a sheet of card, they can start the hole with a bradawl or hole punch and then enlarge it, if required, by pushing a pencil through.
- Cool glue guns: these are used for fixing wood, card and plastic. Children must be supervised while using these, and although the guns produce a cool stream of glue, make sure that children do not touch the glue with their hands. This will help them to begin to appreciate that glue guns can cause burns; this is important as later in their school career they will use hot glue guns.
- Needles, used for working with fabrics including embroidery and stitching: young children may find threading needles quite difficult, so use ones with larger eyes. Needles need to be used with care, as pricks from a needle can lead to infected wounds. Make sure that all needles are collected in again after use and that if children need to leave the sewing table for a short while that their needles are put in a safe place. Again, left-handed children may need extra support as they will sew from left to right, whereas right-handers sew from right to left. It is helpful to show children how to sew using the same hand that they would, and this will need practice for the way you do not normally use.
- Cooking equipment including bowls, wooden and metal spoons, weighing scales and cooking utensils: when working with food ingredients children must take care to ensure the product is hygienically prepared. They need to work in a safe and clean environment, wear aprons which are used just for cooking activities and use utensils with care, particularly knives when ingredients are cut. Children will need to be reminded of health and safety measures which they must follow in order to ensure that risks, such as those associated with using knives, are reduced to the minimum and that hygiene rules are followed. (See Chapter 3 for further detail on health and safety issues.) There are various types of scales for weighing, including dial, digital and balance beam with weights. Whichever type is used, children may need to be shown how to use them, including reading from a dial. Always ensure that the worksurfaces are protected when hot items, such as baking tins, are placed on them.
- Gardening tools including spades, forks, trowels, hoes and plant pots: when working in the garden, children should wear strong shoes to avoid accidents to their feet. Make sure that they do not leave gardening tools lying about as this can lead to accidents. When they have finished their gardening tasks, the children should clean the tools and put them away safely.

Activity 8.2 Using materials and tools Find out which construction kits are used at school. Look at the instruction manual and check that you know how to fit the pieces together. If there are diagrams for making models, make up some of the models so that you become familiar with how the pieces fit together.

Working with children Some construction kits, such as Quadro, make large models and need to be used in a large space as the models will be large. Others can be used on table tops or a carpeted area of floor. Some kits have activity cards and teachers' notes which suggest models which can be made. Younger children may find following the picture instructions too difficult. Older children should be encouraged to find the kit pieces needed for the model before they begin and to match each piece to the picture so that they recognise where it fits. Construction kit activities in the classroom will involve just a small group of children as there will be insufficient pieces for everyone to use at the same time.

Supporting designing

The assistant's role in working with children as they develop their designing skills is to support them as they work. Support includes asking questions, demonstrating a new skill, showing how to hold and use a tool safely, and asking open-ended questions which encourage children to think about the appropriateness of what they have planned and ways in which they can develop their ideas. Children should always be encouraged to attempt a new task or develop a new skill for themselves; it is not appropriate to do the task for them as they watch. In design, children should be encouraged to develop each of the following skills:

- To draw upon their own experiences to help them to think of ideas. These ideas may come from home experiences or from work that they have already done. As time passes they will experience a wider range of materials and begin to know and understand about some of the properties of these materials. For example, younger children will begin to understand how to make stronger structures because they have made models and structures with construction kits and bricks and have some good ideas about which shapes to choose to make a strong base for a model house.

- To discuss their ideas with others in order to clarify their thinking. Talking through ideas with each other and with an adult allows children to share ideas and to discuss a range of ways of tackling a problem. Discussion also helps children to become familiar with and use new vocabulary in context. In supporting discussion, questions should allow children to develop their thinking, rather than rely upon 'yes' and 'no' answers:
  - 'What will it do?'
  - 'Who will use it?'
  - 'How large should it be?'
  - 'What other materials could you use?'
  - 'How will you make it?'
  - 'How will it work?'
  - 'What if ...?'

- To develop their ideas through using the materials. This will involve shaping, assembling and rearranging materials and components. Sometimes the materials to be used will already be given, for example, if children are working from an activity card that suggests the materials and asks them to develop the design. At other times children will choose their own materials, and the adult can encourage them to consider whether their choice is suitable and whether there are other materials which would be more appropriate. Questions to ask include:
  - 'What other materials could you use?'
  - 'Is there another way?'
  - 'Which do you prefer?'

Figure 8.5 A child's sketch of his designs

- To develop their design ideas and communicate them to others by making freehand drawings and draft models. Children can sketch the ideas they have discussed so that they have a clear view of how the finished model will look. They can make draft models, using the actual materials and components with temporary fixings. As they work, encourage them to think about the appropriateness of their design by asking questions such as:
  - 'What materials will you use?'
  - 'What else could you choose?'
  - 'Will it be strong enough?'
  - 'How can you make it stronger/taller?'

- To make suggestions about how to proceed with their designs. Here children will consider how to organise their work. Some questions to ask include:
  - 'What will you do first?'
  - 'Then what will you do?'
  - 'Where will you work?'
  - 'Who will you work with?'
  - 'What will each of you [in the group] do?'

- To consider their ideas as these develop, and identify strengths and weaknesses in their designs. This is part of the evaluation process which will continue throughout the task, from the earliest stages of design to the finished project stage. Through continuing evaluation, children have the opportunity to improve their design so that it is fit for the purpose. Some questions to encourage evaluation include:
  - 'What does it need to do?'
  - 'How will it work?'
  - 'What other materials could you use?'
  - 'What would make it better/stronger?'

Activity 8.3 Lunch bags Design a lunch bag that you might use for your packed lunch. Make a sketch of your design, showing its dimensions and the materials you would use. Show your sketch to a friend and discuss the appropriateness of your choice of design and materials.

Working with children In order to make your sketch you may find it helpful to make a mock-up of your design. This is a technique that you can try with the children. In your discussions with a friend consider whether you were encouraged to respond at some length or whether you replied with a simple 'yes' or 'no'. Open questions encourage a more considered response and give opportunities for the discussion to open up new possibilities for design. If possible, ask the children you work with to design their own lunch bag, and provide them with paper for sketching and a range of materials so that they can make a mock-up of their design if they wish.

Supporting making

From their design, children will make a model. It is the assistant's role to support them as they work, including asking open questions, demonstrating a new skill and checking that the choice of tools and materials is appropriate. (See Chapter 4 for further discussion on open questions.) Do not do the work for them, even if what they produce is untidy, badly cut-out or unlikely to work as intended. Children will only develop their skills of making when they become confident and competent at the skills involved for themselves. In making models children should be encouraged to develop each of the following skills (from Key Stage 1 Programme of Study).

- To select materials, tools and techniques. The range of materials and tools should be carefully controlled so that children have a reasonable range from which to make their choice. They should be encouraged to consider the properties of the materials and how they will work their chosen material. Considerations will include which tools will be needed for measuring, cutting and joining. Some questions to ask include:
  - 'Which material will be strong/bendy/stretchy enough for your design?'
  - 'Which tool will you need to do that?'
  - 'How will you join the pieces together?'
  - 'How will you make the pieces the right size?'

Figure 8.6 Measuring and cutting

- To measure, mark out, cut and shape a range of materials. Some children will benefit from being shown how to use a ruler, matching the start of the measure to one end of the material, and then how to mark the material in order to cut in the correct place. In food technology, children may need help with weighing out ingredients, identifying the measure on the dial, or finding the correct combination of weights to use with a balance. They may need to pour out some liquid into a measuring jug, and may need help to find the appropriate measuring mark on the scale. Marking could include making a pencil mark on the place where a hole must be punched, or drawing around a paper or card pattern or template. In cutting and shaping children may use scissors for paper, card or fabric, or a hacksaw for wood or plastic. Accuracy in measuring, cutting and shaping skills improve with practice; children will benefit from cutting out themselves. Questions which will help them to consider how they will approach the task include:

- 'How will you measure that?'
- 'How could you make it the correct size?'
- 'How do you know you have enough?'

- To assemble, join and combine materials and components. When using construction kits, children will push or 'click' the pieces together to produce their model. Sheet and reclaimed materials, such as cardboard, cartons and tubes, may need to be fixed by gluing, and children may need support when using a cool glue gun or glue stick so that they spread the glue thinly and evenly. Fabric pieces may need to be sewn together. Many children find sewing a complex skill to acquire, as they try to make stitches that are even and neat. They may join two pieces of card using a stapler and may need assistance with placing the stapler at the appropriate point on the card. Joining two pieces of wood may involve using hammer and nails or screws and a screwdriver. Safety considerations must be paramount and children taught to take care when they cut, stick and join. Ask them:

- 'How will you join those together?'
- 'Is there another way?'

- To apply simple finishing techniques. Such techniques include painting a model, covering with coloured paper, adding sequins and glitter to a decorative card, icing some cakes, glazing a clay model or using PVA glue to glaze it if it has not been fired. The surface on which they work should be protected, or use a wipe-down table top. Encourage the children to discuss how they will finish their model and the effect that they want to produce. Provide encouragement and support by asking questions:

- 'How could you decorate it?'
- 'What materials do you need?'

- To make suggestions about how they can proceed. Encourage them to think about what they will need, in what order they should do things, and to consider how they will complete a section before they start, so that they consider what may be difficult before they begin. This will encourage them to become more organised in their approach to their work, to think ahead and to develop independence. Ask the questions:

- 'What materials will you need?'
- 'Which tools will be best for that?'
- 'How will you join those pieces together?'
- 'What will you do first?' 'Why?'
- 'How will you do that?'

- 'How could you make it look better?'
- 'How could you make it stronger?'

• To evaluate their products as these are developed, identifying strengths and weaknesses. As they work, encourage the children to discuss what they are doing and to consider how their model could be improved. Ask questions such as:
  - 'How well does it work?'
  - 'How could you improve it?'
  - 'How does it taste/feel/fit?'
  - 'What would make it even better?'
  - 'What other materials/tools/fixings could you have chosen?'
  - 'Would these have made it better?'

Figure 8.7 Encourage children to clear up as part of the designing and making process

Activity 8.4 Class picnic Design and make some sandwiches for a class picnic. Make a list of ingredients and tools that you will need. Evaluate the finished product and consider how it might have been improved.

Working with children This activity involves the whole process of designing, making and evaluating. At any point in the process it may become apparent that there are design or making flaws and an evaluation of the process at that point will help to identify issues and for new plans to be made. This is an essential part of the design and making process for children. As they become more confident with their skills of designing and making, encourage them to consider, at any point in the process, whether their plan needs to be modified or improved. The picnic activity can be carried out with children in the classroom. Consider how you might modify this to suit the age and ability range with which you are working. Younger children may need help with organising their work systematically. Following written instructions helps children to understand that work in progress needs to be carried out in a systematic way.

> **Making sandwiches**
>
> You will need:
> • Bread   • Butter   • Paste
> • Knife   • Plate
>
> 1. Spread some butter on two slices of bread.
>
> 2. Spread some paste on one piece of bread over the butter.
>
> 3. Put the two pieces of bread filling sides touching to make the sandwiches.
>
> 4. Cut the sandwich into quarters and put these on to the serving plate.

Figure 8.8 Written instructions to be followed systematically

Building key concepts

Developing knowledge and understanding

We live in a technological society, and studying design and technology helps children to make sense of the world around them. They will begin to learn about how things work as well as how to make them, and to evaluate products to appreciate their quality and usefulness. They are expected to develop knowledge and understanding about the following.

- Mechanisms. They will use simple mechanisms, including wheels and axles, perhaps from a construction kit, and make moving joints using simple techniques such as fastening with brass paper fasteners. This helps them to appreciate how moving parts work and to incorporate these ideas into their own designs. Questions to ask include:
- 'How does it work?'
- 'How is it fixed?'
- 'How does it move?'

Figure 8.9 Observation of how parts fit together

- Structures. As they build models children learn about stability, such as building a house with bricks and ensuring that the walls will support the roof. They will learn how to make structures stronger, using techniques such as folding paper into a concertina to make a bridge span which will support greater loads. Experimentation with different materials will help children to begin to appreciate their properties. Encourage children to consider:
  - 'How can this be made stronger?'
  - 'How can it be made more stable?'
  - 'How can it be altered so that it will hold heavier loads?'

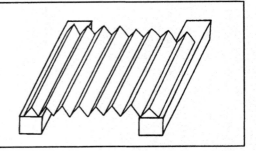

Figure 8.10 A bridge span made using folded paper

- Products and applications. They will learn, by taking simple products apart, how these are made. For example, children might take apart some packaging to see how it was folded and to consider whether the manufacturer had used the minimum of material to keep costs lower. They will consider how materials and components have been used and whether the product is helpful for people's needs, and may ask others to evaluate their usefulness. They might ask questions including:
  - 'What materials have been used?'
  - 'How is it fixed together?'
  - 'How well does it work?'

- Quality. Children need to consider quality in their own work, as well as when they look at manufactured items. They need to think about how well the product fits the purpose for which it is made as well as how well made it is. For example, they might consider whether a new toy is suitable for young children. Questions they might ask include:
  - 'Is it attractive?'
  - 'Is it safe?'
  - 'Is it durable?'
  - 'Will it be considered interesting?'
  - 'Is it well made?'
  - 'Does it do what it is supposed to do?'

- Health and safety. Children need to know how to use materials and tools safely so that they avoid accidents to themselves, others and to their environment. It is still the adult's responsibility to ensure the children's safety and that health and safety rules are followed, but children should, as they mature, take increasing responsibility for considering their and other's safety. This is included as part of the science Programme of Study, 'Science in everyday life', which applies across all other science Programmes of Study. Health and safety considerations include those for working with food. As they plan their work ask:
  - 'How can we make this safe?'
  - 'What are the rules when using ...?'
  - 'Why are these rules so important?'

- Vocabulary. Children need to know the names of tools and materials and to be able to describe techniques using the appropriate language. Always name new tools or materials and use these words in discussion with children. When children discuss their work, encourage them to use a wide range of design and technology vocabulary so that they become familiar with it and understand its meaning. Ask:
  - 'What materials will you use?'
  - 'Which tools will you need?'
  - 'How will you fix these together?'

Activity 8.5 Commercial packaging Choose an example of commercial packaging, such as the wrapping on an Easter egg. Consider these points:
- What is the purpose of the packaging?
- How effective is it?
- How might it be improved?
- Take it apart: how is it constructed and does it represent good value for money?

Working with children Children make informal evaluations of products throughout their lives. They will comment upon new, popular toys and describe their advantages, or talk about a present that did not live up to expectations such as the toy which broke on its first day of use, or the one that soon became boring because its play possibilities were so limited. Helping children to evaluate products in an objective way and against criteria which they can develop themselves helps them to begin to understand about consumer rights and expectations.

Notes to leaders

- ☛ Using a commercial design and technology scheme, encourage assistants to find and discuss activities which promote work in particular aspects of designing, making and improving knowledge and understanding.
- ☛ Provide some materials and tools and, with the assistants working in twos, ask them to match the tools to the materials, then to identify the safety considerations for each pairing.
- ☛ Provide examples of children's sketches for a design. Ask the assistants to evaluate the sketches and decide how they would help the children to improve on their design.
- ☛ Provide examples of models made by children. Ask the assistants to evaluate the models and decide how they would help the children to evaluate and improve their finished product.

Supporting understanding

Resources for working with children

Chadwick, E. (1990) *Collins Primary Technology*. London: Collins Educational.
Gilbert, C. (1989) *First Technology*. Harlow: Oliver and Boyd.
Harrison, P. and Ryan, C. (1990) *Technology in Action. Key Stage 1: Infants.* Dunstable: Folens.

Further reading

CLEAPS: various guides.
The Design and Technology Association (1996) *Primary Design and Technology: A Guide for Teacher Assistants*. Wellesbourne: DATA.
Pitt, W. and Boyle, D. (1992) *S.T.E.P. 5 to 16 Design and Technology*. Cambridge: Cambridge University Press.

ACTIVITY SHEET 1

Working in partnership

Think about your work in the classroom. Write down:
- those things you do well;
- aspects of your work where you feel confident;
- aspects of your work where you need some help.

I do these well ...	I am confident about ...	I need help with ...

Discuss your responses with your teacher so that you can become even more helpful in the classroom.

ACTIVITY SHEET 2

Observation

Observe the children as they choose their activities. Which aspects of gender bias can you see? Complete this chart from your observations.

	Girls only	**Boys only**	**Girls and boys**
Which activities do the children choose?			
Which materials do the children choose?			
Which activities are dominated by particular groups?			

© Montague-Smith, Winstone

ACTIVITY SHEET 3

Risk assessment in the home

Look around you at home and complete the chart.
- What hazards can you see?
- What is their risk?
- What action should you take to minimise the risk?

Hazard	Risk				Action
	None	Low	Med.	High	

© Montague-Smith, Winstone

ACTIVITY SHEET 4

Risk assessment in the school grounds

As you walk around the school grounds fill in this chart.
- Write where you are standing in the 'Area' column.
- *Give a brief description of any potential hazards which you spot.*
- Identify whether the level of risk is low, medium or high.
- Note the safety measures which you would wish to take in the 'Action' column.

Area	Hazards	Risk level	Action

Use another copy of this sheet to note hazards, levels of risk and actions you would take inside school.

© Montague-Smith, Winstone

ACTIVITY SHEET 5

Living or non-living?

Look at the lists and decide for each item whether:
- it is living;
- it has never lived;
- it was once alive.

Write each item into a column below.

Car	Acorn	Flower
Feather	Housebrick	Shell
Can	Cat	Paint
Cotton bedsheet	Lightbulb	Window
Orange	Book	Timber hut
Hairbrush	Comb	Saucepan
Gas	Computer	Leaf
It is living	**It has never lived**	**It was once alive**

Can you find some more items to add to each list?

© Montague-Smith, Winstone

ACTIVITY SHEET 6

In which group do these belong?

Put the animals into their correct groups.
Use the classification chart on page 57 to help you.

Tortoise	Crocodile	Snail
Beetle	Spider	Earthworm
Trout	Stickleback	Blackbird
Frog	Newt	Snake
Whale	Dog	Human
Horse	Starfish	Penguin
Flea	Cow	Caterpillar

Invertebrates (without backbones)	Vertebrates (with backbones)				
	Fish	**Amphibians**	**Reptiles**	**Birds**	**Mammals**

Can you find some more animals to add to each list?

© Montague-Smith, Winstone

ACTIVITY SHEET 7

Solids, liquids and gases

You will probably have some of these in your home.

Fizzy drinks	Salt	Orange juice
Coffee granules	Cooking oil	Washing-up liquid
Tomato sauce	Soap	Air freshener spray
Vinegar	Flour	Chocolate
Cheese	Sugar	Spray polish

In which group would each of these belong? Write them into the table below.
Some examples may go in more than one column.

Solid	Liquid	Gas

Can you find some more items to add to each list?

© Montague-Smith, Winstone

ACTIVITY SHEET 8

What's cooking?

What happens when these foods are heated?

Food and method of cooking	What happens? Colour? Texture?	Is this a temporary or permanent change?
Boiling an egg		
Melting butter		
Heating cooking oil		
Boiling potatoes		
Frying bacon		
Frying chips		

When ice pops are frozen does this produce a permanent or temporary change?

© Montague-Smith, Winstone

ACTIVITY SHEET 9

Does it dissolve?

You will need six cups or clear plastic containers, with the same amount of water in each.

Add one teaspoon of each substance to a cup.
Does the substance dissolve in water? If not, try stirring it.
Put the results into the table below.

Substance	Dissolved without stirring	Dissolved with stirring	Did not dissolve
Coffee granules			
Tea leaves			
Sugar			
Salt			
Flour			
Cooking oil			

© Montague-Smith, Winstone

ACTIVITY SHEET 10

Electrical conductors and insulators

Set up an electric circuit with a 4.5V battery, 3V bulb and three wires with crocodile clips, leaving a gap between two of the wires for the test item. Try the different materials as part of *the circuit* to see if they are conductors or insulators.

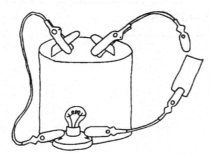

Material	Does the bulb light up when the material is in the circuit?	Is the material an insulator?	Is the material a conductor?
Wool			
Plastic			
Steel			
Fabric			
Iron			
Wood			
Paper			
Graphite (pencil lead)			
Copper			

Find some more examples of conductors and insulators.

© Montague-Smith, Winstone

ACTIVITY SHEET 11

Forces in the home

Think about pushes and pulls that happen in each of these activities.
Write a sentence to describe each activity using the words push and/or pull.

Activity	Description
Getting dressed in the morning	
Opening a cupboard door	
Closing a drawer	
Sweeping up leaves in the garden	
Writing the letter a	
Walking across the floor	
Moving a doll's pram	
Opening an umbrella	

In which other activities do you use pushes and/or pulls?

© Montague-Smith, Winstone

ACTIVITY SHEET 12

Thinking about light sources

A group of children gave the following examples when asked to suggest light sources.

Torch	Christmas tree lights	Mirror
Bedside lamp	Kitchen spotlight	Stars
Television	Sun	Moon
Sparkling jewels	Glow-worms	Cats-eyes in the road

Which of these actually produce light?
Which reflect light from other sources?

Produce light	**Reflect light**

Find some more examples to add to each list.

© Montague-Smith, Winstone

Bibliography

Association for Science Education (1990) *Be Safe!* Hatfield: ASE.
Association for Science Education (1994) *Safety in Science for Primary Schools*. Hatfield: ASE.
Bentzen, W. (1997) *Seeing Young Children: A Guide to Observing Behaviour*. New York: Delman Publishers Inc.
Chadwick, E. (1990) *Collins Primary Technology*. London: Collins Educational.
Crawford, M., Kydd, L. and Riches, C. (eds) (1997) *Leadership in Teams in Educational Management*. Buckingham: Open University Press.
Creary, C. and Wilson, G. (1996) *You, Me and Us*. Northampton: Northamptonshire Science Resources.
The Design and Technology Association (1996) *Primary Design and Technology: A Guide for Teacher Assistants*. Wellesbourne: DATA.
DFE (1995) *Key Stages 1 and 2 of the National Curriculum*. London: HMSO.
Dunne, D. (ed.) (1996) *The New Sc1Book*. Northampton: Northamptonshire Inspection and Advisory Service.
Farrow, S. (1996) *The Really Useful Science Book*. London: Falmer Press.
Fisher, J. (1996) *Starting from the Child*. Buckingham: Open University Press.
Fox, G. (1993) *A Handbook for Special Needs Assistants: Working in Partnership with Teachers*. London: David Fulton Publishers.
Gilbert, C. (1989) *First Technology*. Harlow: Oliver and Boyd.
Harlen, W. (ed.) (1985) *Primary Science: Taking the Plunge*. Oxford: Heinemann Educational.
Harlen, W. (1996) *The Teaching of Science in Primary Schools*, 2nd ed. London: David Fulton Publishers.
Harrison, P. and Ryan, C. (1990) *Technology in Action. Key Stage 1: Infants*. Dunstable: Folens.
Hughes, C. and Wade, W. (1991) *Bright Ideas – Inspirations for Science*. Leamington Spa: Scholastic.
IChemE and NIAS. *Health and Safety Activities Box*. Northampton: Northamptonshire County Council.
Kennedy, J. (1997) *Primary Science: Knowledge and Understanding*. London: Routledge.
Morris, J. (1996) *Themes for Early Years – Growing*. Leamington Spa: Scholastic.
Moyles, J. R. (1992) *Organising for Learning in the Primary School*. Buckingham: Open University Press.
National Curriculum Council (1993) *Teaching Science at Key Stages 1 and 2*. York: NCC.
NIAS (1996) *All Sorts of Stuff*. Northampton: Northamptonshire Inspection and Advisory Service.
NIAS (1996) *Chemistry and Cookery*. Northampton: Northamptonshire Inspection and Advisory Service.
NIAS (1998) *Push, Pull and Twist*. Northampton: Northamptonshire Inspection and Advisory Service.
Nuffield (1995) *Primary Science Teachers' Handbook*. London: Collins Educational.
Nuffield Primary Science (1997) *Understanding Science Ideas*. London: Collins Educational.
Patterson, J. (1996) *Schools Organic Gardens*. Hatfield: The Association for Science Education.
Peacock, G. and Smith, R. (1992) *Teaching and Understanding Science*. London: Hodder and Stoughton.
Pitt, W. and Boyle, D. (1992) *S.T.E.P. 5 to 16 Design and Technology*. Cambridge: Cambridge University Press.
Richards, R. (1989) *An Early Start to Nature*. Hemel Hempstead: Simon and Schuster.
Richards, R., Collis, M., and Kincaid, D. (1990) *An Early Start to Science*. Hemel Hempstead: Simon and Schuster.
School Curriculum and Assessment Authority (1997) *Baseline Assessment Scales*. London: HMSO.
School Curriculum and Assessment Authority (1997) *Looking at Children's Learning: Desirable Outcomes*. London: SCAA.
School Curriculum and Assessment Authority (1996) *Nursery Education: Desirable Outcomes for Children's Learning*. London: HMSO.
School Curriculum and Assessment Authority (1995) *Science: Consistency in Teacher Assessment. Exemplification of Standards. Key Stages 1 and 2, Levels 1 to 5*. London: SCAA.
SPACE (1992) *Reports of the SPACE Research Project*. Liverpool: Liverpool University Press.
Wade, W. and Hughes, C. (1991) *Inspirations for Science*. Leamington Spa: Scholastic.

Useful addresses

Anything Left-handed, 20a New Street, Worcester WR1 2DP. Tel: 01905 25798.
Association for Science Education (ASE), College Lane, Hatfield, Herts AL10 9AA. Tel: 01707 267411.
Child Accident Prevention Trust, 4th floor, Clerks Court, 18–20 Farringdon Lane, London EC1R 3AU. Tel: 0171 608 3828.
CLEAPSS, School Science Service, Brunel University, Uxbridge UB8 3PH. Tel: 01895 51496.
British Gas Education, PO Box 70, Wetherby, West Yorkshire LS23 7EA. Tel: 01937 843141.
British Heart Foundation, Education Department, 14 Fitzhardinge Street, London W1H 4DH. Tel: 0171 935 0185.
Friends of the Earth Trust, Information Department, 26–28 Underwood Street, London N1 7JQ. Tel 0171 490 1555.
General Dental Council, 37 Wimpole Street, London W1M 8DQ. Tel: 0171 486 2171.
The Design and Technology Association (DATA), 16 Wellesbourne House, Walton Road, Wellesbourne, Warwickshire CV35 9JB. Tel: 01789 470007
Health Education Authority's Primary School Project, Thomas Nelson and Sons Ltd, Nelson House, Mayfield Road, Walton-on-Thames, Surrey KT12 5PL. Tel: 01932 25211.
Heron Educational Limited, (Primary Science and Technology Equipment), Carrwood House, Carrwood Road, Chesterfield S41 9QB. Tel: 01246 453354.
Learning through Landscapes, Third Floor, Southside Offices, The Law Courts, Winchester, Hampshire SO23 9DL. Tel: 01962 846258.
National Dairy Council, Education Department, 5–7 John Princes Street, London, W1M 0AP. Tel: 0171 499 7822.
NES Arnold Limited, (Primary Science and Technology Equipment), Ludlow Hill Road, West Bridgeford, Nottingham, NG2 6HD. Tel: 0115 945 2200.
Northamptonshire Inspection and Advisory Service (NIAS), The Science Centre, Spencer Centre, Lewis Road, Northampton NN5 7BJ. Tel: 01604 756134.
Pedigree Petfoods Education Centre, 4 Bedford Square, London WC1B 3RA. Tel: 0171 255 2424.
RSPCA, Head of Education, Causeway, Horsham, West Sussex, WR12 1HG. Tel: 01403 264181.
Royal Society for the Prevention of Accidents, Edgbaston Park, 353 Bristol Road, Edgbaston, Birmingham B5 7ST. Tel: 0121 248 2000.
Royal Society for the Protection of Birds, Head of Education, The Lodge, Sandy, Bedfordshire SG19 2DL. Tel: 01767 680551.
Sherston Software Ltd., Angel House, Sherston, Malmesbury, Wiltshire SN16 0LH. Tel: 01666 840433.
Technology Teaching Systems Limited, (Primary Science and Technology Equipment), Monk Road, Alfreton, Derbyshire DE55 7RL. Tel: 01773 830255.
Understanding Electricity, 30 Millbank, London SW1P 4RD. Tel: 0171 344 5839.

Index

assessment observations 7, 13
assistants in the classroom 5–14
attitudes to science and design and technology 24
children's recording 17
communication 6–7, 39–50
confidence 50
curriculum: right of access 10–11
design and technology 18–19, 23, 79–91
   and the National Curriculum 18
   assembling, joining and combining 87
   children's early experiences 79
   definition 18–19
   designing 18, 23, 84–5
   evaluating 18, 85, 88
   health and safety 19, 21, 90
   knowledge 18, 19, 89–91
   making 18, 23, 86, 87
   organising work 85
   products and applications 21, 90
   quality 21, 90
   materials, tools and techniques 80–85
   skills 18, 19
   structures 21, 89
   supporting children in 84–9
   understanding 19
   vocabulary 21, 42–3, 90
   working systematically 87, 88, 89
Desirable Outcomes 3, 20, 21
equal opportunities 10–12, 25
   English as a second language 11
   gender and learning 10, 24–5
   special educational needs 10
equipment 18, 19, 25
first aid 27
health and safety 5, 6, 10, 11, 26–38, 53, 55, 57, 58, 62, 63, 64, 65, 67, 71, 76, 81–4, 87, 90
information technology 4, 6, 16
   CD-ROM 16
   safety when using computers 33
   software 46, 47–50
   word-processing 46, 47, 50
investigations 22–3
key concepts 2, 3, 20, 51–9, 60–68, 69, 70–78, 79, 89–91
life and living processes 51–9
   children's early experiences 51–2
   green plants as organisms 55–7
   humans as organisms 54–5
   knowledge and understanding 21
   life processes 52–3
   living things in their environment 57–8, 59
   variation and classification 56–7
materials and their properties 60–68
   children's early experiences 60–61
   changing materials 63–8
   collections 63
   chemical changes 65, 66–8
   dissolving 66–7
   evaporation 66, 67
   grouping materials 61–3
   heating 65
   natural and synthetic 66

physical changes 66, 67
   properties 61
   solids, liquids and gases 63–5
   solvents 66–7
   thermal conductors and insulators 61–2
   water 64, 65–66
National Curriculum 15, 18, 20–21
parents and carers 50
physical processes 69–78
   changing shape 75–6
   children's early experiences 69–70
   electrical conductors and insulators 71–2
   electricity 70–73
   floating and sinking 73–4
   forces and motion 73–6
   friction 74
   light 76–7
   magnetic forces 76
   making circuits 71–2
   mass and weight 73–5
   pushes and pulls 69, 73, 75–7
   sound 77
   starting and stopping 75
planning 12–13
play 22
processes in learning 2
practical work 22
problem-solving 23–4
Programmes of Study 20–21
questioning 8, 9, 10, 43–5, 62, 84, 85, 86, 89, 90, 91
   closed questions 43–4
   making predictions 8–9, 41
   open questions 8, 9, 43–5
research skills 16–17
resource management 5
risk assessment 26–8, 30, 37–8
   risks 26, 30, 31, 32–3, 33–4, 35, 36, 37
role of the assistant 5–12
   planning 8, 11–12
   preparation 8, 12
   supporting the children 7–12
   supporting the teacher 5–7
   vocabulary 8
school policies 5, 6, 27, 54, 81–2
science 15–18
   and the National Curriculum 15
   equipment used in science 17
   investigating 16–17, 22
   knowledge, skills and understanding 16–17
   what is science? 15–18
science and design and technology 1–2, 15–25
   and adults 1
   attitudes to 24–5
   children's developing interests 1–2
   Desirable Outcomes 20
   gender and learning 24–5
   hypotheses 19
   investigations 19
   knowledge and understanding 21
   National Curriculum 20–21
   processes in 20
   relationship between 19

scientific learning 19
   skills 21–5
   solving problems 19
   using scientific knowledge 19
   what children learn 20–21
science skills 17, 21–2, 42
   considering evidence 21–2
   discussing 17
   drawing 19
   fair and unfair testing 21, 41
   investigating 21
   observing 16–17
   obtaining evidence 21
   planning 16, 21
   recording 17
   safety 17
   using secondary sources 17
supporting children 8–12, 40–50
   children making choices 10
   children's ideas 39–41
   considering evidence 42
   demonstration 8, 11
   designing 42–3
   developing questioning skills 43–5
   developing thinking 45–6
   displays 46, 49–50
   encouragement 9–11, 88
   discussion 8–9, 11, 12, 39–41
   explanations 8, 11
   evaluating 43
   fair testing 41
   forming positive relationships 10–12
   giving feedback 9–10
   helping children with their work 10
   making 42–3
   nature of special educational needs 10–11
   obtaining evidence 42
   organisation 8, 11
   plan, do and review 40
   praise 9, 10, 11
   prediction 39, 40
   processes 39
   recording outcomes of work 46–50
   showing children what to do 8–12
   using IT 46–50
   variables 42
   vocabulary 8, 10, 11, 12, 41–3
teachers supporting assistants 12–14
   assessment observations 13
   evaluating 14
   expectations 12–13
   planning time 12
   review of working practices 13–14
   verbal feedback 12–13
   working together 12
   working with children 13
   written working agreements 14
technological advances 19
using mathematical skills 41, 43, 82
vocabulary 41–3
   for science and design and technology 21, 41–3, 90
   for supporting children 8, 9, 10, 11